Erin —

May unending hope be
your guide.

"It's rare when a storyteller uses multiple mediums to communicate a thought or message, but that is exactly what Nikole Lim does in *Liberation Is Here*! Using powerful words and visual imagery, she becomes a storyteller of transformation–both hers and others–to make us see faith in new ways. Liberation isn't for some; it's for all. Liberation isn't far away; it's here and now."

Bianca Juarez Olthoff, writer, pastor, and author of *Play with Fire*

"Nikole Lim's *Liberation Is Here* is the story of three African women, all of them sexually assaulted as children, and their extraordinary journeys to survival, restoration, and leadership. Their unforgettable stories convey the appalling reality of near-total impunity enjoyed by men who rape children. Ms. Lim finds hope in the breathtaking courage of rape survivors whose suffering has compelled them to advocate on behalf of others."

Gary Haugen, CEO of International Justice Mission

"What a vulnerable, deep, and profound book of hope and hidden beauty! Through the lens of an artist, in powerful and beautiful images, Nikole Lim's *Liberation Is Here* stewards the stories of women who have survived abuse and sexual violence. Heart-wrenching and full of trauma, the accounts of violations against women are not the end of the story. Rather, Lim walks the reader through a transformative journey of joy and profound pain in the quest for liberation from sexual violence and oppression. *Liberation Is Here* describes a mutual process of transformation and liberation where our individual freedom is bound up in the stories, pain, and the triumph of others' quests for redemption and healing. Lim describes how healing and transformation parallel the story of Jesus through joy and pain, death and rebirth. May all who read *Liberation Is Here* experience the binding power of our common humanity as we hold onto hope and seek mutual healing and justice."

Mae Elise Cannon, author of *Social Justice Handbook* and *Beyond Hashtag Activism*, executive director of Churches for Middle East Peace

"*Liberation Is Here* captivated me right from the start and left me feeling inspired and changed. Nikole's story and the stories of those she encounters in her journey stretch our minds and hearts, helping us to see possibility in our pain and realize truths that unite us and set us free. Join me in reading it again and again."

Nicole Zasowski, marriage and family therapist, author of *From Lost to Found*

"With unflinching honesty yet gentle compassion, Nikole Lim draws close to women who live under oppression, shame, and gender-based violence. But she also treats her subjects as more than victims. Rather, women like Nekesa, Mara, and Mubanga have something to teach any reader about their own pain and oppression, and show that liberation comes not through avoiding brokenness but by moving through it with the mercy and love of God."

Katelyn Beaty, author of *A Woman's Place: A Christian Vision for Your Calling in the Office, the Home, and the World*

"Nikole Lim shares words, images, and stories that moved me to tears. However, they were tears of joy as I embraced these powerful narratives of resilience and hope. These amazing women show us that while it often feels so far from us, if we truly see the people around us, they are everyday reminders that *Liberation Is Here*."

Jonathan "Pastah J" Brooks, pastor of Canaan Community Church, Chicago, and author of *Church Forsaken: Practicing Presence in Neglected Neighborhoods*

"*Liberation Is Here* gives so much hope to all who question their ability to overcome adversity. Nikole Lim paints a picture of strength and God's overwhelming love for humankind. It is a testament of faith that transcends culture, economic status, and race. As women, each of us can see ourselves. I was captivated by each and every word and reminded of how resilient we truly are when we allow miracles to overtake us."

Sha' Givens, author, minister, humanitarian

"In *Liberation Is Here* Nikole gives us a vivid and inspiring lens on what it's like to walk alongside those who are marginalized in their pursuit of liberation. These are stories of hope serving as evidence that healing happens when we are courageous enough to move beyond our comfort zones and do something that terrifies us in the beginning. Both compelling and convicting, the stories Nikole shares about serving with survivors of sexual violence not only allow a glimpse into the lives of these amazing young women but encourage us to look at ourselves and ask hard questions about our willingness to trust God amid what may appear to be impossible odds. *Liberation Is Here* is just that, powerful proofs through stories about what it looks like when people are willing to do the uncomfortable, hard work of healing. This is not just a book about what it takes to help heal others. As humbling experiences with the 'oppressed' expose our wounds, Nikole allows us to see what happens when we realize that we are also in need of healing."

Romal Tune, author of *Love Is an Inside Job: Getting Vulnerable with God*

"Nikole Lim's journey is a reminder of the power of storytelling. It highlights critical elements, such as the importance of establishing a person's safety, the integrative function of narrating trauma in this safe environment, and the importance of meaning making and relationships in healing from trauma. I experienced a whole range of emotions–crying, laughing, cheering, anger–reading *Liberation Is Here*. This book helped me reprocess many personal and client experiences. Thank you for sharing your story, Nikole. This is a must-read for anyone working with survivors of trauma!"

Lubi Kwendakwema Zulu, clinical psychologist

"Nikole Lim allows us to see into a world foreign and distant to many of us. . . . With the telling of every story she allows us to find our calloused hearts loosened. There are no easy answers here, but we find ourselves as in her words, beginning to allow ourselves 'to love amidst difficult places.' Thank you, Nikole, for taking us into the places where God can ask us, 'Where are you?' This is a profound telling of story, and Nikole's is a profound work in the world."

Juanita Campbell Rasmus, spiritual director, copastor of St. John's United Methodist Church, Houston, and author of *Learning to Be: Finding Your Center After the Bottom Falls Out*

"*Liberation Is Here* is painfully and beautifully written. At various points while reading the book, I would clutch my shirt, gently moving my hands over the left side of my chest where my heart is . . . as if to reassure myself that although these stories might hurt, they are not only stories about pain. In some of the most harrowing stories, I was forced to permit a smile and appreciate the precious and sacred nature of what was being shared. This book is a reminder that the work of justice and healing is as much a personal and internal journey as it is a sociopolitical and external journey. Perhaps the greatest offering that Nikole and the Freely in Hope scholars give us is their commitment to telling the truth, even when it is does not look, sound, or feel good. The truth-telling in this book is not simply a matter of facts to be repeated but also of authority to be reclaimed, joy to be rediscovered, self-ownership to be exercised, and the kind of generosity of spirit that only healing healers can offer. It is a privilege to endorse this labor of love by Nikole Lim."

Lovelyn Nwadeyi, social justice activist and strategist, South Africa

"Nikole Lim uses her skills as a filmmaker and invites us to see with our hearts and minds what liberation could look like on earth as it is in heaven. Lim challenges us to see and name the brokenness not as an abstract concept out there but within the world we live in and in our own lives, and it is beautiful, haunting, and convicting."

Kathy Khang, speaker, activist, and author of *Raise Your Voice*

"For all those working for a more just and beautiful world, this book is a must-read. In the stories of survivors, you will recognize your own story. You will find not only practical lessons for leadership but the presence of joy, freedom, and radical imagination–the presence of God."

Rebecca Ume Crook, survivor and cofounder of Metis, Nairobi, Kenya

LIBERATION
IS
HERE

WOMEN UNCOVERING HOPE
IN A BROKEN WORLD

NIKOLE LIM

An imprint of InterVarsity Press
Downers Grove, Illinois

InterVarsity Press
P.O. Box 1400, Downers Grove, IL 60515-1426
ivpress.com
email@ivpress.com

InterVarsity Press® is the book-publishing division of InterVarsity Christian Fellowship/USA®, a movement of students and faculty active on campus at hundreds of universities, colleges, and schools of nursing in the United States of America, and a member movement of the International Fellowship of Evangelical Students. For information about local and regional activities, visit intervarsity.org.

While any stories in this book are true, some names and identifying information may have been changed to protect the privacy of individuals. The people portrayed in the images do not correspond with the stories depicted in this book.

Cover design and image composite: David Fassett
Interior design: Jeanna Wiggins
Images: woman silhouette: Nikole Lim
        storm clouds: © Xuanyu Han / Moment Collection / Getty Images

All photos are used courtesy of the author.

ISBN 978-0-8308-3185-2 (print)
ISBN 978-0-8308-3186-9 (digital)

Printed in the United States of America ♾

Library of Congress Cataloging-in-Publication Data
A catalog record for this book is available from the Library of Congress.

P 25 24 23 22 21 20 19 18 17 16 15 14 13 12 11 10 9 8 7 6 5 4 3 2 1
Y 41 40 39 38 37 36 35 34 33 32 31 30 29 28 27 26 25 24 23 22 21 20

DEDICATED TO MY GUNG GUNG

who told me to write before I knew how.

CONTENTS

INTRODUCTION

MY LIFE'S EXPERIENCES
are like photographs—where dark and light, sun and shadow
collide to create stories forever burned in my retina.

When I first started playing with a Canon Rebel XT, one of the
first models of consumer digital single-lens reflex cameras (SLRs),
I learned how the settings determine the amount of light that
reflects through the lens. The higher the shutter speed, the less
light that enters in, and the lower the aperture, the more light that
enters in. Shooting at the lowest aperture setting, or shooting
"wide open," concurrently means shallow depth of field. I love
using this technique when taking portraits—focusing in on the
face so that everything else blurs, bringing only the person into
focus. Shooting "wide open" allows me to capture the diverse
beauty of people's faces, laden with untold stories, while soft-
ening the distractions of the background, bringing their humanity to the forefront.

As a filmmaker and photographer, I have worked with international organizations to capture stories of people around the
world, from fathers recovering from drug addictions in the city of
Los Angeles to children caring for elders afflicted with leprosy in
the jungles of Vietnam. Their stories of triumph amid oppression
challenge me. After every photo session, I often show them their
portraits to ensure they approve. I hope that they see themselves
the way that I see them: strong, radiant, full of dignity despite the

labels that may have been placed on them. I love seeing their eyes light up as they look at their image. "Am I really that beautiful?" they ask. I love uncovering the hidden things of their story that help them discover beauty in themselves—beauty that they never saw before.

My work in photography and film has allowed me to experience stories not my own. But when I was invited into stories told by survivors of sexual violence, my work took an unexpected turn. I began to recognize that there were many limitations in my work. Before then, I didn't know that the capacity of my heart was small—unable to comprehend the depth of love that I experienced in community with survivors. Through their stories they taught me what beauty, redemption, and healing look like. By allowing my heart to be "wide open," I experienced limitless hope in a broken world. There, my own journey toward healing began to unfold.

This is a story of my struggle for liberation and the oppressed who unexpectedly liberated me in the process.

This book follows the stories of three survivors of sexual violence: Nekesa, Mara, and Mubanga. (Some names and identifying details have been changed to protect the privacy of individuals.) Their vision for a world free of sexual violence challenged me to change my career and start Freely in Hope, a nonprofit organization that equips survivors and advocates to lead in ending sexual violence. As the survivors in our community evolved in so many ways, Freely in Hope also evolved to support their audacious dreams by expanding its support to fund holistic education, leadership development, and storytelling platforms that seek to prevent sexual violence in communities across Kenya and Zambia.

The monstrosity of these traumatic stories may be triggering. At the same time, exposing these stories is a gesture of pulling back darkness to bear witness to light. This book is an attempt to tell stories that have expanded my heart's capacity to find love amid my most difficult experiences. As the stories of these survivors have intertwined with my own, I now see the world as a strange juxtaposition—the unfolding of beautiful things from desolate places. I have learned to not only shoot "wide open" but to also keep my heart wide open by experiencing the hope that arises from the brokenness of our world. Their journeys toward transformation also transformed me.

This book is for world changers, countercultural leaders, and perspective shifters—dreaming of the day when liberation is a fully embodied experience for all of humanity suffocating under the weight of oppression. For the little girl imprisoned in the city's brothels, for the young man afraid to verbalize the abuse of his boyhood, for the father relentlessly advocating for the rights of his child, for the mother caught in a cycle of no options, for survivors who are blamed for crimes they did not commit: let us move toward liberation together.

My hope is that in these stories you may see a glimpse into the possibilities of your own story—

that hope is ever present in the midst of despair,

that healing emerges from brokenness,

that suffering has the potential to expand our heart's capacity for love,

that liberation arises from places of violent oppression.

May these stories be an invitation to experience the world through a new perspective—recognizing that liberation is not just near, it is here.

If you have come here to help me,
you are wasting your time.
But if you have come because your
liberation is bound up with mine,
then let us work together.

LILLA WATSON

one

SHE REMINDS ME OF YOU

My MOTHER'S FATHER GREW up in the village of Gungyi, hearing the roaring sounds of Japanese jet fighters, the crescendo of explosions, and the rainfall of debris. As a freelance journalist, he published an article that was falsely accused of criticizing communism. It put him on the list to be killed. His friend, a communist soldier, secretly told him that he must flee immediately, lest he be killed by morning. My grandfather escaped to Hong Kong and later immigrated to San Francisco where he built a growing church over the course of thirty-five years. After that, he chose to go back to serve as a missionary to the remote villages of China. His experiences there opened my eyes to a world beyond the confines of Richmond, the California suburb where I grew up.

When my grandfather was a missionary in China, he would often send me photos of the people he served in hidden mountain villages. Ethnic minority tribes were shunned to rural regions to live in perpetual poverty while the rest of China prospered below. Despite food scarcity and lack of government concern for the people, his photos showed children playing, women laughing, and men engaging over cups of tea. His photos were vivid— displaying expressions of joy and stories of hope. These stories, however, were also infused with issues my young mind could never comprehend. Oppression, imprisonment, and affliction were so foreign to my carefree childhood.

In his photos, the Bai peoples were adorned with white clothing embroidered with fuchsia hues the shape of blooming camellias. Red and white tassels dangled from their headdresses to frame their faces. During celebrations, it was colorful and vibrant, my grandfather wrote. But most of the time, while working in the fields, they wore traditional cotton garments that were black, the color of suffering.

From my grandfather's stories, I grew up understanding there was a larger narrative that spanned the complexities of oppression and poverty. In it was a constant thread of dignity woven throughout the silk brocades of stories that have shaped mine. Through his images I observed how dignity—the quality of being worthy of honor—remained, even in suffering.

When I was eleven, my grandfather sent me a photo of a little girl from a village. Her home was carved out of the sides of the cold mountains. She looked like she was around the same age as I was. She looked painfully shy, with a sadness in her eyes that told an unspoken story. My grandfather titled this photo: "She reminds me of you."

I had the haunting realization that this little girl could have been me.

◆　✳　◆

Growing up, I was immersed in unspoken cultural expectations simply by being a girl. I was expected to be docile, submissive, and quiet, accepting what is without raising questions or causing conflict. Expressing anger, or any strong emotion, was considered weakness. Emotions were to be controlled, not communicated. Chinese women often display the pretense of perfection in public while criticizing our flawed humanity in private. Believing humility is the same as humiliation, we use words to humiliate ourselves before someone else can.

But I possessed none of these qualities. Too many times I have opened my mouth uninvited, laughing too loudly or reacting with anger when my mother darted her piercing eyes at me and muttered, "That's not ladylike." Everything I said or did was expected to represent my family with honor. Not wanting to bring them shame, I concealed my emotions, from joy to rage. I wasn't allowed to express them fully. I quickly learned that I must conform if I were to belong. My body hunched over, anger clutched at my heart and inhibited its expansion to feel something more.

As a child, I was keenly aware of my family's immigration story. My grandparents escaped war, famine, and poverty in pursuit of new opportunities for generations to follow. I had no choice but to succeed in order to keep our family out of poverty. Doing otherwise would dishonor the risks my grandparents had taken in their brave mission across the Pacific Ocean. My parents took up house-cleaning and grocery-bagging jobs to get through university. Through education, they moved our family out of poverty within one generation. I had the same pressure to succeed academically and financially. However, being third generation in America, I had the privilege of pursuing any dream I desired—as long as it led to a financially viable career. "I created you to be better than me," my mother would often say.

As a teenager, I began to understand how the little girl in my grandfather's photograph could have been me. I wondered why I was lucky enough to have been saved from a life of poverty, to have an abundance of resources available to me, and to have access to quality education that would bring me closer to the dream I desired. Yet I struggled with how to reconcile the success of my parents with the poverty of my grandparents. I questioned my role, wondering what responsibility I held due to the privilege of being born third generation. Though I escaped what could have been, my bloodline carried a narrative that was still true for so many. The image of the little girl in China haunted me in my sleep.

This struggle is what sparked my interest in documentary film-making. I imagined how telling a more uplifting narrative of those who have experienced oppression could bring about liberation.

I wanted my work as a filmmaker to change how these stories were told, highlighting strength and stamina beyond desperation or despair. Contrary to what was depicted in mainstream media, I knew these stories existed because of what I had been told by my ancestors. They were stories of joy and resilience laden with violence and war. While hardship may have been constant, hopelessness certainly was not.

Angry with the way people of color and people in poverty were depicted in film and television, filmmaking became my outlet. It was a way of voicing my opinion without being verbal. My anger translated to silence. In my early teens, I started creating documentary films to earn income by capturing stories in my neighborhood, on Skid Row, and eventually on the playgrounds of our ever-expanding world. I enjoyed hiding behind the camera, giving voice to a more engaging story than my own. I was incredibly idealistic, hoping that my career in filmmaking could cast light on the untold stories of the world.

But as I listened, I discovered that it was more than my small heart could hold.

I listened to the child in the Los Angeles foster-care system as she described the captivity of repeated sexual abuse after moving from house to house. She fought back tears in an attempt to prove that the abuses of power could not take away her freedom.

I listened to the story of a woman afflicted with leprosy and ostracized to a fishing village in the southernmost tip of Vietnam. With damaged fingers, she shared her hopes for her son as she lovingly prepared rice noodles topped with fresh herbs for him. Her son, however, did nothing to support her health in return.

I listened to the teenage girl who escaped the brothels of Kolkata as she expressed her gratitude for freedom to work where she chose. She served me chai, sugared to perfection. With both hands extending the tin cup to me, I saw that her golden bangles hid freshly cut lines of dried blood.

While every story of pain beckoned me to enter in, I dared not. For me, capturing these stories was a way of hiding—disengaging from my own pain and connecting with someone else's. As they cried tears of sadness, I refused. Showing my own emotion was weakness, I had been taught to believe. At the same time, I viewed the people as incredibly strong for being able to do so themselves. It was a freeing experience for them. But I couldn't allow myself to feel for fear of finding something of darkness within me.

The shadow of my former self
follows me wherever I go.

As I go, I take a part of her with me—
but only the parts that I choose
to recreate into something better.

For in reaching back into the shadows
to bring her out into the light,
our liberation will begin.

And although the shadow of my former self
threatens to haunt me by night,
she must flee by day.

For the overwhelming light of the world
dispels all fear of my shadow,
my former self,
my darkness
that I secretly carry within.

She is always present—reminding me of failures
I
dare
not
repeat.

She, however, must stay behind me.
For it is her existence that is making me into the light
I am becoming.

two

A COMMON THREAD

I WAS TWENTY YEARS OLD when I first met Nekesa. I landed in Kenya to capture stories for my thesis film about women who inspire hope in their communities. A friend invited me to sit in during her university class to learn more about the challenges women face in Kenya. She told me there was a girl in her class that might be a good fit for my thesis film.

Nekesa was out of breath as she flung open the door to the classroom. Her pant legs were dusty and her braids were coming out. She found her seat at the front just as the conversation was about to begin.

"What are some issues that women face in our communities?" the teacher asked.

Nekesa was the first to raise her hand. She stood to speak: "In slum areas—especially here, in Kenya—men take advantage of the poverty of women. This is why we see so much rape, incest, and prostitution in our communities." She paused to swallow, "This is why I'm here—to help survivors find their healing."

Her whispery voice pulled me in to listen. She spoke with such assurance that I was eager to learn more from her.

As we left the university together, mamas were selling Maasai earrings for 200 shillings ($2.00) outside the university gate.

"Sister, look here! I'll give you two for 300," the mama said.

It was an offer I couldn't resist. "Nekesa, do you want a pair?" I asked.

"Ah! No. I would much rather use that money to buy unga for my baby," Nekesa said. Unga is the cornmeal used to make ugali, the staple food in Kenya.

Stunned, I quickly learned that she and I had vastly different priorities. Feeling guilty, I took her into a supermarket, and I said she could get a few things. She only asked for a small packet of unga, a bar of soap, and a toothbrush. As we spent time together over the course of the month that I was in Kenya, a friendship began to form. I asked if I could interview her for my thesis film, and she enthusiastically agreed.

On our scheduled day of filming, I set up my equipment in a quiet corner outside her university. Shaded from the heat of the noon sun, she began to share her story with me.

"I was born in Ebutayi, a small village in the western part of Kenya. When a girl is born, there is a big celebration. The whole village comes together and the women will dance and sing and cry ululations. But even though the village celebrated my birth, the celebration would last much longer if I were born a boy," she began.

At eighteen, Nekesa had dreams of going to college, but being a girl, she was expected to sell mandazi, breakfast fritters, on the side of the road to support her family of thirteen. Her father, a day laborer, and her mother, a maize farmer, were at odds about allowing their daughter to go to college. Most of the girls in her village were already married, pregnant with a second child, and dropping out of school to tend to the domestic needs of their husbands. Nekesa was able to finish both primary school and high school, resisting the expectation of marrying early. As a high school graduate, the bride price would be raised—instead of one cow, she could be worth three. Her father saw it as a benefit for himself, but the idea of allowing his daughter to go to college was senseless.

"I wanted to go to Nairobi to look for work so that I could pay for my university tuition. But my father wanted me to get married. He believed that I would be worth nothing more than dowry to him. My mother, the only person who believed in my dream, told me to go."

Her mother blessed her by spraying spittle on her face and chanting prayers of safety for her journey ahead.

With only bus fare in her pocket and the few items of clothing she owned, Nekesa jumped on a matatu, a bus, painted "Nairobi" in red letters. She planned to meet a distant relative in the Mathare slum when she arrived.

"Going to Nairobi for an education seemed like an impossible dream for me," Nekesa recalled—remembering when she was a young schoolgirl dashing through fields, scattering grazing impala. Her primary school crammed over one hundred students from multiple grades into one space. Each grade turned their wooden benches to face a different iron sheet wall. There was no blackboard, no chalk, no textbooks, just stubby pencils they clutched to copy assignments into their notebooks. Students competed for attention, snapping and calling, "Teacha! Teacha!" As her fellow students stood to speak, the bench would suddenly tip over like a seesaw. She quickly learned to balance her weight. Nekesa competed to be the top of her class.

"But now, I was imagining myself running through a crowd of university students to get to my classroom," she said. She would find her seat at the front and sit up straight. There would always be enough chalk, and she would be surrounded by knowledge and the prospect of a career that would allow her to be a woman with purpose in this world. Rather than imprisoned in a thatched-roof house she would be free to stride the halls as an educated woman. "I dreamed of how I would even greet my professors in perfect English, the kind with a British accent," she laughed.

The dream was getting closer and closer as the matatu sped past Nakuru's rock formations. The boulders emerging from the soft green grass looked like the backs of hippopotamuses resting in the water. Her eyes rested with them.

Eight hours passed. Nekesa awakened, startled at the sound of buses honking. People patterned with colorful kitenge climbed in and out of the buses. Hawkers waved bananas and roasted maize in front of bus windows to seduce passengers with a snack. Young men carried bags of tropical mints for five cents in one hand and a bucket of mandazi for ten cents in the other. Women held crates full of glass Coke bottles on their heads splashed with water to make them look cold.

"I was in shock," she told me. "I had never seen so many people in one place before—Nairobi was only a place in my dreams." Surrounded by buses and concrete towers, Nekesa surveyed the organized chaos in the Railways Terminus. She stepped off the matatu and asked people where the bus to Mathare was. Most of the people ignored her question, but finally a well-dressed man approached Nekesa and asked, "Did you say you're going to Mathare? I'm heading that way too, I can take you." With relief, Nekesa thanked him, happy to have found a bit of kindness in this unfamiliar city. He spoke in Luhya, her mother tongue, and mentioned places and things that were familiar to her in Ebutayi. "We're like brother and sister!" he laughed.

When they arrived in Mathare, he let Nekesa use his phone to call her distant relative. There was no answer. "Why don't we go to my place while we wait for your relative to call you back? I can make supper." Nekesa enthusiastically agreed. She hadn't eaten all day, since there was no food in the house when she left. While preparing to cook ugali with mrenda and chicken, he served her a glass of orange Fanta. Nekesa finished the glass in a few gulps. They continued to share common stories of Ebutayi.

"At first, I felt like I was in the right place. But then I started to get dizzy. I didn't understand what was happening to me, and I fell asleep," she said as she shook her head in disbelief.

As she paused, my stomach tightened. I distracted myself by double-checking my camera to make sure she was still in focus. She continued her story.

Hours later, Nekesa's eyes opened wide. Curtains closed. Body naked. Pain. Sheets covered in blood. He was reclining next to her.

"What did you do to me?" she asked.

"Isn't it obvious? You're in my house, I can do whatever I want to you. Now hurry up! Get your filthiness out of my house. If you tell anyone that you were raped, trust me, I will kill you!"

Rape. Nekesa couldn't believe that this could happen to her. "In my culture, I grew up learning that sex is only reserved for your husband. The boys in my community learn about their sexuality through ritual ceremonies that prepare them for manhood. They have the right to have sex with their wives whenever they wish. But for girls, we were only taught to keep quiet and do what they want. But this stranger was not my husband, so I knew that this was very wrong!" she said with certainty.

The man took her back to the matatu stage—the same place where he had tricked her into trust. As passengers boarded the matatu to Western Kenya, he grabbed her elbow with a twist. Nekesa opened her mouth to scream, but fear silenced her. He pulled her close and whispered, "Remember, I will kill you." He shoved a 500-shilling ($5.00) note in her hand, just enough for a one-way ticket home.

"On the bus, I cried throughout the long journey home. I felt so alone—no one on the bus bothered to look at me or help me," Nekesa's throat tightened. I tried to think of some comforting response, but the words would not come. I did not know how to hold the heaviness of her story.

Arriving at her family home, she was met not with comfort but with sneers.

"Eywe! You are very stupid to think you can go to the universities with the big, big people. If we couldn't go there, what makes you think you can? Girls can only bring home cows, not a degree!" When her father yelled at her, his breath smelled of busaa, the local brew homemade from fermented maize.

"I didn't even think I was worth a cow," Nekesa said. "Now I was 'used,' so no man would pay a dowry for a girl who was not a virgin. I couldn't let my father know what had happened in Nairobi. The rejection I faced at home made me want to give up—in a way, it felt worse than being raped by a stranger," she said as her eyes moistened. She closed her eyes, allowing her tears to fall, feeling the weight of rejection compressing her chest. I felt it too, but I held back my own tears. I was angry—imagining how I would feel to be rejected by my family for something I did not do.

Ridiculed for returning to the village as a failure, Nekesa gave up her dream of a university degree and followed in her mother's footsteps farming maize. One day, while working the fields in the hot sun, she threw up. Her mom, watching her closely, asked, "Are you pregnant?" Nekesa was defensive. "How could I be when I've never slept with any man?" But her mother knew just by looking at her—something had been broken in her daughter's body, which also broke her spirit. But they never spoke further of it. Afraid to recognize the truth, they would rather hide what would bring them shame.

The words of the rapist, "Remember, I will kill you," stayed with her, along with his seed. Nekesa was afraid that if she spoke up, the rapist would kill her—if her father didn't kill her first. She hid her secret for as long as she could, until her belly began to swell, showing evidence of an unspoken sin. When her father noticed her bulging belly, he accused Nekesa of being a promiscuous slut.

"Eshitwatsi! I did not raise a prostitute in my house! Never come back here again!" screamed her father as she fled.

With nowhere to go, she returned to the same slum she was raped in to start a new life, hoping to create one better than what her father damned her to. Pregnant and underweight, she went from house to house asking for work. Sometimes she would be paid 100 shillings ($1.00) to hand wash a large load of laundry. Other times she would be paid 200 shillings ($2.00) to sweep the house, scrub the walls, and wash the curtains. She would fetch water and wash cars for a nearby car mechanic for 50 shillings ($0.50).

"All of my money went to pay rent. I didn't have enough food to eat, so I begged from the people I cleaned for," she said. She ate any food offered to her by clients and leftover communion wafers from the Catholic parish nearby.

As Nekesa continued to share, the overwhelming emotions that she had suppressed caused her to shake. She left the room weeping, leaving me alone with my camera. I was stunned, unsure if I should continue or not. After some moments, she came back and sat in silence.

"Would you like to take a break?" I asked.

"No," she responded, "I need to tell you what happened next. I thought, how could I give birth to this baby if I can't even afford to feed myself? I decided to get an abortion." She saved up 600 shillings ($6.00) to have an abortion in the so-called clinics that are operated by avafumu, witch doctors and medicine men. She waited in the damp, dark room underground, staring at the faces of other women who probably found themselves in similar circumstances. She wanted to ask them questions and listen to their stories to find some sense of hope, but she kept her mouth shut, afraid to tell her own. Since abortions were illegal in Kenya, witch doctors and medicine men profited from unsafe procedures. Many girls have died from bleach intoxication, profuse bleeding caused by wire hangers prodding their uterus, small bottles filled with explosives completely rupturing the uterus, or a traditional concoction of strong tea leaves and gasoline.

A man wearing a lab coat that was no longer white and smudged with blood stains said, "Next." It was her turn. An overwhelming fear rose in her. Too many of her friends had died from abortions such as these. She turned to the woman beside her and told her to go ahead. "Then, I heard the voice of God tell me, 'This baby is going to be a blessing to you.' I didn't understand how, but fear of dying came over me, and so I left the clinic."

When it was time to give birth, she had just the 200 shillings ($2.00) needed to deliver at the hospital. Despite not having any food in her system, her frail body gave birth to a healthy child. "Here is your beautiful girl!" said the doctor with excitement.

Nekesa was surprised at the doctor's choice of words and thought, *Beautiful? Something beautiful could come out of me?*

As Nekesa talked about her beautiful baby girl, her shoulders lifted and her eyes glistened with affection. A feeling of hope began to rise within her. I felt it too. I looked at her in awe, enamored at how pain and beauty could both exist in her body.

"I tied my baby to my back with kitenge and had to hustle. I washed laundry, cleaned houses, fetched water, and washed cars, doing anything I could to buy unga," she said. She raised her baby in the slums, struggling to eat enough food to produce breast milk. Some days she would leave her baby with a neighbor only to come back and find her alone, crying from neglect. Looking at her tearful little face, Nekesa resolved to create a better world for her baby girl than the one she was raised in. In prophetic anticipation, she named her Hope.

She told her mom that because of the birth of her baby girl, her dream for an education came back. Her mom labored in the fields and sent her 6,000 shillings ($60.00)—equivalent to gathering 600 pounds of maize. Because her mom invested in her dream, Nekesa vowed to one day build her mom's dream, a house with her daughter's name on the deed. With that and the money from washing cars, she enrolled herself in university.

"My dream is to become a social worker so that when other girls who have been raped see me, they will know that if I can do it, they can too. And that is how I came to the university!" She said, showing off her teeth.

After a month of filming various women throughout Kenya, I returned to Los Angeles to edit my thesis film. I was particularly challenged by Nekesa's story. As I edited, her story played over and over, and a barrage of questions filled my mind:

What would I do if her story were mine?

Would I rebel against familial mandates to pursue my dream?

Would I go against cultural expectations that risked bringing shame to my family?

Would I pursue an unconventional career despite community ridicule?

Would I be brave enough to commit my life to helping others through the same trauma I had experienced?

"She reminds me of you," I heard my grandfather whisper.

It was then that I realized her story could have been mine had I been raised in a different political climate in China, had I been born to parents who preferred a boy as their first child, had my grandparents never fled communism, had my parents been unable to find jobs because of discrimination, and had I not been given opportunities to pursue my academic dreams.

While I was attempting to make a career out of telling other people's stories in the film industry, Nekesa was rewriting her own story. While I was pondering all the ways I could become profitable in Los Angeles, she was trying to put food in her daughter's belly in Mathare. While I was finishing up my final year of university, she was just beginning hers. While I was focused on building my own dream, Nekesa was building a dream for many—starting with her daughter.

I saw how the struggle of my ancestors paved the way for me to write a new story as well. For I too desired to create a better world for my future daughters, should I have any. And if I did, I wondered, what would I want their world to look like? I did not know at the time, but I knew that I had a responsibility to reconcile the suffering of the generations before me. A common dream united Nekesa and me across borders. I paid her balance for the remainder of her semester.

When Nekesa's results came back, she was at the top of her class.

Perhaps our differences could bring us closer together than the pretense of similarities ever can.

three

CAUGHT UNAWARE

Soon after I graduated from college, I was assigned to shoot a story on a church in Kibera, Africa's largest informal settlement. Kibera is home to one million people packed within one square mile. The pastor who hosted me there also ran a primary school for over a hundred children. "Education is very important, but many cannot afford it. Even though government primary schools are free, there are fees for uniforms, pencils, notebooks, and exams cards. We built this school for the babies and when they grew up, we added more classrooms to accommodate them. There are too many children who want an education, but there is no space or resources to build more free private schools."

"What about for high school?" I asked.

He shook his head, "High school is not free in Kenya. There are too many students who can't afford to go. Ah, there's a young girl at my church, her name is Mara, I think you should meet her to learn more. She lives deep inside the slum." His voice lowered as he said it. "To get there, we must climb. Keep your camera inside your bag—be careful," the pastor said as he led me through narrow pathways. We shimmied our way between tiny homes layered with sticks and red soil.

"Many come to Kibera trading the poverty of the village for survival in the city. There is so much hope when they come, but they soon realize that life is very difficult here. Only hustlers survive, while others die from diseases in the water. Crime is everywhere, but people can't go to the police. There is no justice. Here, there is something called 'mob justice,' where a mob of young men will take it upon themselves to kill thieves either by stoning them or burning them to death," he told me.

Land is scarce in Kibera, with houses built adjacent to each other in lines of disarray. Homes are roofed with corrugated tin sheets, rusted until brown, earning Kibera its nickname of the Chocolate City. Rent ranges from 500 to 3,000 shillings ($5.00-$30.00) per month, depending on the size of the house and the fairness of the landlord.

We crossed a broken bridge overlooking a river of gushing water carrying all sorts of debris—this manmade river of sewage flows through Kibera. The debris-filled river is the only source of running water in Kibera. He told me that clean water was imported with trucks. Filling a jerry can of the imported water is ten shillings ($0.10), but it could increase to thirty shillings ($0.30) if there was a water shortage in Nairobi. Since few homes have their own toilet, some dig shared pit latrines within their compound, while others use government-sanctioned toilets at ten shillings ($0.10). Girls using these communal toilets at dark often risk getting raped.

"For people who do not have a toilet or can't afford one, we use a 'flying toilet.' Have you ever heard of that before?" I shook my head, confused. He made a throwing motion with his hand and pointed down to the narrow streets we walked on. They were lined with plastic bags that created colorful patterns in the dirt. I slowed down my pace, even more determined not to misstep and slip.

"So if I am a father with a family of eight and I have ten shillings ($0.10), I have to decide if I will buy water, use the toilet, or buy a tomato so the children can eat something with ugali. It's an easy choice!" he chuckled while I coughed from the smoke-filled air that smelled of charcoal and manure.

The smoke billowed from tiny homes that were converted to bars during the day. They served chang'aa, meaning "kill me quickly," a home-brewed spirit made from fermented grains and often laced with petrol oil or embalming fluid. Men walked around with leather belts hanging from their arms and a string of leather wallets draped around their necks. Women sat by the roadside frying fish, samosas, and mandazi. High school students lined the roads wearing uniforms of all color combinations. White socks and black Bata shoes united them all.

I walked through a group of children skipping throughout the streets. They chanted, "Mzungu, how are you?" in high-pitched unison. Their round faces were framed in white hijabs or knitted caps. The light reflected off their tiny palms as they waved.

I noticed other children who were not wearing uniforms. They helped their mothers in the shop by shredding sukuma wiki, the most common leafy vegetable, and measuring the weight of beans. Shop owners set up their made-in-China plastic wares inside vibrantly colored shipping containers. Used clothes, bought by weight, were displayed in rows and sold at twenty shillings ($0.20) a piece. The sound of buses honking, conductors yelling, children laughing, and radios blaring swelled into a symphony called *home*.

Approaching Mara's home, we ducked under dripping laundry hanging on a line and jumped across inlets of flowing sewage. Here, on a dirt foundation, behind rusty tin sheaths and faded sheets made into curtains, was the home that Mara has lived in since she was eight years old.

Arriving at the doorstep, I started to take my muddy shoes off to leave them outside, but Mara's mom stopped me, "Eh! Don't do that! Come inside! Karibu!" She grabbed me by the shoulders and held me close to one side of her body, then the other side. I could feel the strength in her arms as she greeted me. I took off my shoes anyway.

Their home was a single room—smaller than my bedroom back at home. Two beds, a couch, a chair, a coffee table, a jerry can of water, and a television were strategically placed like Tetris pieces. A floral bed sheet hung loosely from wall to wall, separating the single room into two. The plastic dishes were faded from scrubbing. In contrast to the muddy exterior, their home was immaculately clean on the inside.

The pastor introduced Mara and me, but Mara did not look up when she shook my hand. She was seventeen and approaching her last year of high school. Our differences formed a busy intersection that was hard to cross. She wore an oversized T-shirt and black leggings, sitting on a tiny stool and leaning over her knees. She hid her heart in a protective stance as if she had been violently wounded too many times before.

"My name is Mara. I stay here with my mother, brother, and niece," she whispered. Her voice was so soft that I could barely hear her over the traffic on the roadside.

They were forced to flee Uganda after Mara's father died. Upon his death, everything was taken away by her father's family. They accused Mara's mother of killing him by infecting him with HIV. But she was negative. In retaliation, the family threatened to kill her and the children too if she didn't get off their land. At the same time, Mara's mom found out that they had betrothed Mara to an older man in the community. She was only eight. Her mom couldn't let her late husband's family take captive of her only daughter, and they left as soon as they could to avoid the female circumcision ceremony. This is what brought them to Kibera.

I felt warmly welcomed by Mara's mom as we sat on the couch, our shoulders touching. She suffered from high blood pressure. At dawn, she roamed construction sites selling chai and mandazi to the workers. Mara's oldest brother looked for manual labor jobs but usually returned home empty handed. Her niece who lived with them was her other brother's daughter, whose mother had left her there after running off with another man.

Security was low, and the stakes were high—too many times their family had gone without eating to afford their two-thousand-shilling ($20.00) rent. They would burn sugar in a teaspoon and stir it in hot water for flavor when they couldn't afford tea leaves. They would eat unseasoned cabbage when they couldn't afford salt. If they couldn't afford the cabbage, they would eat the boiled remnants of bitter herbs that grew wildly around the edges of the slums. Mara's mom started to grow a small vegetable garden as a way to earn income.

Mara went to the local government primary school tuition-free, but when she got to high school, the burden of tuition became too great for her mother. Mara took up the night shift at a local pub in Kibera to contribute to her educational dream. As a result, Mara was in and out of high school—constantly being sent home for not paying her school fees. Finally approaching her fourth year, she was desperate to graduate.

I tried to ask Mara questions about her dreams for the future, but she would only answer with a nod and sometimes a quick glimpse into the eye. Most of my questions were answered by her mother, who spoke on her behalf. "She's a very bright girl, she does very well in school, and she's a hard worker! She's just tired today because she works at a restaurant at night."

"Where do you want to go from here?" I asked Mara. She didn't respond.

I was beginning to become irritable at her irresponsiveness. Mara's mom tried to coax her on: "Mara, talk to the mzungu."

Out of obligation, Mara finally spoke: "I want to finish high school. I need to be a role model for other girls like me. The world needs to see what's happening here—we are suffering."

In that moment, I limited myself from learning too much, from asking more questions, from connecting too closely, and from allowing my emotions to get involved in my work. I hardly knew anything about this suffering she spoke of. My twenty-minute hike to her home gave me a glimpse of some of the external challenges. But the internal suffering is what I sensed most in the positioning of her body.

I shot a few photos of the pastor and Mara's mother as they caught up in Swahili. I was hired to capture the success stories of this church in Kibera—the happy children in school uniforms, the people saved at the church altar, and the multitude of families fed rice and beans—not the suffering.

I asked Mara if I could take her picture and she reluctantly agreed. "Smile!" I said, but she refused. "Cheka!" I said in Swahili, and an uncomfortable pursed-lip grin emerged. I turned my camera around to show her my last photo, which caught her chagrin. Despite her timidity and unimpressive rhetoric, I thought I saw a spark that was just waiting to be kindled. "Do you like it?" I asked her. She pulled the corners of her lips down.

I left disoriented, not knowing how to hold all that I had experienced. My journey through Kibera flooded me with guilt, causing me to question why I was lucky enough to have escaped the poverty and violence that led families there. On the hike back through the neighborhood, I tried to comprehend what my role as a photographer was to be. Constantly going in and out of these homes was troubling. Though I was invited in, there was a disconnect that made me question the purpose of my presence in this foreign space. I thought of Mara, wondering what would possibly soften her defenses.

Trudging my way back to the main road, God spoke to me very clearly, saying, "Invest in Mara. She will bring liberation to her community."

The next day I sent her the money she needed to finish her final year of high school. Neither Mara nor I knew what might happen next.

*The oppression of our world
is a mirror to the oppression
within myself.*

*May it bring light to the
darkness that I hide.*

four

WHERE ARE YOU?

W HEN I WAS FOURTEEN, my mom became very ill. While out of town, she bled profusely for over two weeks and lost so much blood that she passed out. She was rushed to the hospital, where tests were run. When we picked her up from the airport, she was in a wheelchair. All color had drained from her body. "What's wrong, Mom?" my little sister, in her innocence, asked repeatedly. We all remained silent as we waited impatiently for the results.

Three days later, I heard my parents sobbing behind closed doors. I knew the answer was cancer.

The thought of losing the person who represented strength to me in a quiet yet powerful way broke my spirit. That night, I hid in my bedroom, and for the first time, I cried out to God, asking, "God, where are you?" I begged for some sense of comfort to cross the distance I felt from God. I couldn't understand how a loving God could allow suffering such as this.

I had come to believe that feeling pain was weak. I had created a version of myself that concealed all feelings to prove that I was strong; to prove that I could withstand pain—even my mother's cancer. However, the thought of losing my mother, the only person who was patient with me in my rage, forced me to access a pain I had never before experienced. Before that moment, I rarely cried or showed any emotion besides anger.

As pain expressed itself in tears, an overwhelming sense of God's nearness came over me, saying, "Because I first loved you, learn to love yourself and others."

I was defensive. I'm supposed to love myself? Despite my angry and bitter heart? In this relentless cycle of shame? In my words of violence? In the way I demean others and myself?

"Because I first loved you, *learn* to love yourself and others."

I did not know what that looked like.

The doctors caught the cancer early enough that she did not need chemotherapy. Since the cancer had not spread, the doctor removed the organ that gave me life. My mother was not the same. She suffered from depression, alternating between sorrow and exasperation multiple times a day. She locked her door, laying in bed most of the day, in the darkness of her room, wondering if she would ever find healing, if she would ever be the woman she once knew. The surgery caused improper healing and the wound became infected. It was a frightful sight, and she wouldn't let me come in to help her clean it.

When the wound started to heal, she slowly began to venture outside of her bedroom. She practiced Qi Gong while facing the wall in her office. Where she used to work long hours creating art, she now created small movements to generate circulation in her body. Breathing steadily, pumping wholeness back into her broken body in an effort to restore her spirit. Exhausted, she went back to her bedroom to hide.

We didn't talk about those emotions. To ask about them would be disrespectful. She would rather mask them lest the monstrosity of it all brought her shame. When her bedroom door was locked, I knew not to knock. Being found in her tears was too humiliating. Instead, I asked what she wanted to eat for dinner. Jook, Chinese conjee, was the common response. I soaked the rice.

This painful process of healing both the outer wound and the inner loss took time. Eventually she began to see the scar on her belly as a mark of survival. As her wound healed, she decided to take her life back. Though she never became the woman she once knew, she became better, recognizing the ways in which beauty arises out of seemingly broken situations.

After my mom recovered, I took up documentary jobs to make ends meet. In addition to shooting for international organizations, I shot weddings to pay off college loans. When an old friend asked me to shoot her wedding in Lusaka, Zambia's capital, I was excited to expand my photography portfolio in a new country.

I stayed with extended family in Chilanga, a crowded township twenty-five kilometers outside of Lusaka. Homes in Chilanga are made of everything from cow dung to cement to bricks, depending on your income bracket. Each morning, hundreds of children dressed in an array of uniform colors walk to school, some for two hours. At one in the afternoon, the children in the morning session walk home, passing another group of children headed to the afternoon session. The nearby government schools are too small to accommodate the growing number of children, so they have two sessions per day. Access to justice is even more scarce, with one understaffed police post to cover the demands of the large township. With little to no financial support from the government, its officers have been known to affiliate with criminals for a portion of the loot.

During the day, women sell mopane worms and kapenta (dried sardines) on the roadside. Men scurry back and forth carrying whatever piecework they found for the day. Small children gather stones and dig a row of parallel holes in the ground to play nsolo. Boys push along their toy cars that they ingeniously made out of soda cans and plastic bottle caps. Girls assume responsibility for duties inside the house—cooking, cleaning, washing, and serving elders. At five in the afternoon, everyone in Chilanga convenes in the market. Women bring out freshly cut vegetables to the market stalls. Teenage girls bathe after a long day's work at home and put on clothes crisp from the drying line. Wrapping themselves in chitenge, they go outside simply to be seen and to buy vegetables for dinner. Teenage boys congregate by the roadside in their skinny jeans and graphic tees, bouncing to music from their phones, flirting with the freshly showered girls passing by. During the night, local bars blast Afrobeats, zed music, and kalindula—music with an eclectic mix of pidgin English and tribal dialects, syncopated rhythms, high-register guitar riffs, and percussion found only in the heart of the diaspora.

Dancing to the distant echo of the beat, the girls of the house where I stayed prepared dinner, fanning the embers glowing on the mbaula, a stove made of clay. Nshima, the staple food made from processed corn flour, is cooked with the strength of the arm and a flick of the wrist. Pumpkin leaves are boiled down and blended with freshly roasted groundnuts pounded into a powder to make ifisashi. They made a red sauce of grated tomatoes, onions, green bell pepper, and an abundance of salt. A whole chicken was killed, cut into small pieces, and deep fried until the skin was browned into a dry crisp. They set the gizzard aside for the father as a symbol of honor, and the girls fought over the chicken heart like my sister and I fought over the wishbone.

Meals are served while kneeling to show respect to elders. As each dish was carried out, the girls kneeled to place the food on the table. They kneeled as they placed a basin on the floor and poured warm water over my dusty hands. They kneeled as they brought a fork for me, unsure if I would eat with my hands.

The children ate on the floor in the kitchen while the adults ate on couches in the living room, quietly watching the news on Muvi TV. I wasn't sure where I was supposed to sit, but I knew I would eat with my hands.

The mother of the house sat me next to her—she is the bread-winner of the family. She sold potatoes to pay for her tuition at secretarial school. Her determination secured her a job as a county government receptionist, where she's been working for the past two decades at the same pay rate. Having three daughters, she committed everything to invest in their education, knowing that higher education would allow them to rise above the poverty they knew. The house she rents in Chilanga was protected by a wall made of bricks with vertical shards of glass and broken bottles lining the top. Outside their gate stood the pit latrine, covered by corrugated tin and shared with six other homes. Within their gate stood a mango tree, its flowers displaying varying hues of yellow and red. With her humble paycheck, she struggled to ensure that her daughters were in school and that their house was safe.

The three daughters are from different fathers: Grace, the oldest, had her mother's sense of humor. Mubanga, the middle child, hid herself in a book when she wasn't fetching something at the shop. Mapalo, the youngest, loved to dance and would incite dance competitions with her older sisters. The father of the house could be found sitting at his sewing machine—but only when he had a special order. Most days, he watched a Nigerian televangelist deliver people from demonic possession.

Their home was always filled with laughter. I wished I understood any of the three languages spoken so that I might learn to laugh as freely as they did. The mom enjoyed cracking jokes, usually making fun of something silly one of her daughters did. When the girls were young, she would ask, "Who broke the plate?" or "Who left this here?" Before any of the other sisters could respond, Mubanga would always yell out, "It wasn't Mubanga's fault!" She referred to herself in third person to prove she wasn't there at the time of the incident. This was still a running joke of the house—if the girls did anything wrong, her mom would say it first, "I already know, it wasn't Mubanga's fault!" But Mubanga would rarely laugh. Soft spoken and reserved, she preferred to sit alone in the corner of the living room. She was just fourteen years old and reminded me so much of myself when I was that age: the insecurity, the attitude, the rolling of the eyes. Or maybe it was the fire in her eyes, the rebellious spirit, or the desire to be free.

I wanted to attempt a friendship with her because I knew that beneath the mask was a story waiting to be told.

I needed to buy a pair of leggings to wear under my skirt for the wedding. My skirt was just above the knee, which would show too much skin for a church wedding. In Chilanga, women wrapped a chitenge around their waists to cover the intersection between their legs to hide any appearance of female sexuality, or they might be indicted for seduction. Mubanga's mom asked her to take me to look for leggings in town. Before we left, Mubanga's mom tied a chitenge around my waist as Mubanga tied one around hers.

On our way to the bus stop, we passed rows and rows of colorful shops painted with logos and popular brands. Tables built from recycled wood and branches displayed everything from tomatoes and kapenta, bitter herbs and smoked sausages, spare auto parts and petrol oil displayed in glass bottles.

"Uncle, muli bwanji? Auntie, muli bwanji?" Mubanga would greet all elders, cupping her hands into a soft clap and curtsying.

"Wow, you know everyone!" I exclaimed, trying to get some response from her.

She shrugged, "I don't. In my culture, I was taught to greet my elders to show them respect."

When we arrived at the Kulima Tower bus station in town, I was overwhelmed by the number of buses and people scurrying across intersections. Not knowing where I was going, I walked cautiously, bumping into people and almost getting hit by a bus in the process. The driver honked at me and angrily yelled, "China!" Mubanga grabbed my hand to guide me through the chaos and maneuvered through the masses to arrive at the Kamwala Market. She was always a few steps ahead of me, while I scrambled along behind her. If she reached for my hand, I didn't reach back—I didn't want to show that I needed her help.

Mubanga pointed to a shop where leggings of all colors were hanging from the ceiling. I found a pair of black leggings that would do.

"Three hundred," said the shop owner.

"No, it's not," Mubanga retorted.

With arms crossed and sass in her voice, she bargained hard for those black leggings. She shook her head, unimpressed, until finally she nodded her head and motioned to me to pay. I was impressed with her stubbornness, which got me a fair price of 100 kwacha (around $8.00).

That evening, Mubanga asked, "Will you escort me to the salon?" We walked to the salon just a few shops away from home.

"Auntie, muli bwanji?"

"Ndiri bwino. Kaya inu?" said the hairdresser, who was putting the last row of box braids into another customer's hair.

"Bwino. This is the weave I'm wearing for my uncle's wedding tomorrow."

"Who's this?" the hairdresser asked, pointing with her lips.

"She's only here for the wedding," Mubanga said with certainty.

"Mmm," she sang as she raised her eyebrows to greet me.

The hairdresser sectioned parts of Mubanga's hair and used a hairdryer and hair pick to comb them out—combing and blowing, combing and blowing. She braided cornrows in lines from the top hairline to the base of her neck—twisting and pulling, twisting and pulling. With a needle and thread, she stitched the weave onto the cornrows. The hairdresser spoke in Nyanja as Mubanga responded with sing-songy *mmms* and staccato *ahs*. Two hours later, she was transformed. She looked so much older in this up-do weave.

Walking back home in the dark, she put her hand in mine and leaned in close, our shoulders touching.

"My stomach is in pain," she whispered.

"You must be hungry. It's dinnertime."

"No, it hurts like this every day . . . since last year. It's a really sharp pain, as if someone is stabbing me."

"Have you ever gone to the clinic to get it checked?"

"Yes, but that was last year. I'm fine. Forget about it," she said as she let go of my hand.

I stopped to look her in the eye. Her eyes diverted from mine.

With a sigh to muster up courage, she began, "I'll tell you my story—but I hope that you will understand."

The stomach pain started six days after her thirteenth birthday. Mubanga was preparing for school that morning. "Eat some nshima before class," her mom said as she wrapped a scarf around her shoulders.

"I'm running late," Mubanga said as she quickly tied a chitenge around her waist and dashed out the door.

She walked the same path to school every morning, reciting the periodic table of elements in her head with each step. Just as the front gate of her high school was in sight, three men approached her. One man said, "Come with us now, otherwise we will kill you." He revealed a knife and pressed it against her belly. Because they were much older than her, she followed, for she was taught to respect her elders through submission. She was afraid of being punished by the knife if she refused. She silently followed them to a gravesite. Hidden beneath mango trees, the man with the knife raped her while the others watched, waiting for their turn. He used her chitenge as a rug to keep his legs from getting dirty. He choked her to keep her from screaming. He kissed her, and she quickly turned her head and saw a metal car part on the ground. She reached for it and swiped it across his face.

She ran home without looking back. They ran after her, attempting to gang rape her, but she miraculously escaped from their hands.

Arriving home, her mother was surprised to see her, "What are you doing here? Was class canceled?"

Mubanga shook her head.

"Were you chased from school?"

"Was the teacher on strike?"

"Are you sick?"

"Did someone make fun of you?"

Every question her mother asked was met with a shake of the head.

"Did someone hurt you?"

Mubanga nodded her head.

"Where does it hurt?"

Mubanga was ashamed to respond.

"Were you raped?"

They wept.

They filed a report at the Chilanga Police Post. There were two police officers there, both male. Mubanga's mom reiterated the story to the police. Afraid, Mubanga could not look at the men; their very presence made her body shake with anger. She told the officers that she remembered exactly what the rapists looked like— she'd seen them before at the local bar as they got drunk by morning.

"What were you wearing? Were you really walking to school or were you going to their place? Is one of them your boyfriend?" Not believing her, the police told her to go to the hospital for a report. "Prove to us that it was rape," they told her as she left.

At the clinic in Chilanga, she was met with the same insensitive questioning and invasive probing. They brought the hospital report back to the police proving that she was raped. Uninterested, the police told them they had to wait for another similar report before they could file a case against these known men.

Weeks passed, and they never heard back from the police. On her way home from work, her mother inquired daily. It seemed cruel to wish that another rape report would be filed, for Mubanga's mom would never wish for such a thing to happen to anyone, even to the woman who ran away with her ex-husband. Mubanga's playful and childlike spirit had been taken away from her. She jumped at every sudden sound. She prayed for invisibility when men passed by. Her walk to school was a daily reminder of a crime she did not commit.

The memory of the rape replayed over and over in her head, but she was not allowed to speak of it. She had been warned many times by her family, "Don't talk about it, otherwise no one will want to marry you." It could never be mentioned, for it was too shameful to be spoken about.

Silenced, she grew angrier by the day. Her stomach pangs increased from her unspoken trauma. She numbed her pain by coming home drunk. At church, she sang loudly, allowing the tears of shame to mask as tears of worship. While her family joked with her, she forced herself to laugh along. But her laughs did not emerge from the pit of her belly, where the pain remained. It escalated into sleepless nights where she felt hands crawling on her skin and saw shadows of three men passing by her window. When she closed her eyes, the rapist was staring back at her.

Tormented by unspoken shame, Mubanga thought that she was unworthy of life. She wished that the men had killed her with those threatening knives. Instead, she was left to suffer for a violent attack that was not her fault. Or was it? She was wearing a chitenge as she had been taught, but perhaps this was punishment for sins of the past. Perhaps God did not love her enough to save her. Perhaps she should have listened to her mom by eating the nshima before going to school. Perhaps she shouldn't have followed the men in the name of respect. Perhaps it was she who brought this on herself.

Bearing a burden of pain so great, she thought the only means of escape was death. She swallowed a handful of malaria pills and waited to die. Nothing happened. If the rapist wouldn't use the knife against her, then she would. She put a deep cut into her wrist.

Mubanga finally looked back at me. There were no tears. She held her hand out for me to hold. Her eyes pointed to the scar on her wrist. I did not know what to do.

This time, she waited for a response from me. I had none, so she took my hand in hers.

It was not your fault, I wanted to say. But the words would not come.

That night, I hid in the bathroom and wept, allowing my tears of anger to collide with the warm water I dumped over my head. I splashed water on my aching body to hide the sound of my sobs. I had captured many stories of violence across the world, but none that I identified with in this way. None that opened up to me without obligation. None that became family. None that I was beginning to love.

Searching for answers, for some semblance of hope, for the presence of God in this pain, again I asked God, "Where are you? You who are all-loving, compassionate, merciful, and gracious, where are you in the brokenness of the world? Where are you in the lives of little girls who are suffering from violence? Where is your protection over your children, God? Where are you?" In the silence, I felt that God was turning those questions on me:

Where is your love for my children?
Where is your compassion for the innocent?
Where is your mercy for the poor?
Where is your grace for the exploited?
Where is your protection for the oppressed?
Where is your justice for the abused?
Where are you?

As I've asked this question of God so many times, I am softly reminded by God that he is there. In the tears, in the pain, in the woundedness of our world, God is here.

The next morning, we all piled into the back of a box truck on the way to the wedding. An auntie started to sing, her voice resounding in the box truck, and everyone responded in tandem. Mubanga lifted her voice with them, singing all that she was not allowed to say, conversing with God in melodies translated by the divine. They told stories of pain and joy in the tenor of their voices, which crescendoed to meet the heavens above, resolving into warm chords that promised something of hope. For a moment I was lifted from the grief of the night before.

The wedding was a beautiful celebration of love. I ran around the whole day, trying to capture everything that I witnessed. As the women danced, they tied chitenge around their hips, highlighting the movement of their waists. Mubanga danced with her whole heart, and it was then that I finally saw her come alive. Dance was her outlet—her way of expressing her pain. She danced until she was out of breath, reminding herself that she was still alive. Though her spirit was broken, her body was not. Rather, her body was unquestionably strong with the capacity to move with power, authority, and freedom.

She reached out to invite me in, but I pointed to my camera to signal that I had to take pictures. My body doesn't express itself in that way—or I refused to allow it to.

But for her, something seemed to loosen when she danced.

Upon leaving Zambia, Mubanga hugged me tighter after I let go. As she held on to me, I suddenly felt very afraid for her. Her daily walk to and from school was a constant reminder of her trauma. She said, "Do you know what stopped me from taking my life? After I cut myself, I realized that my blood was the blood of Jesus. Because he loves me, I need to love myself and others. I'll see you when we finally meet with God one day." Neither of us imagined that we would see each other again.

Overlooking the dry desert landscape of Lusaka as my plane took off, something loosened in me too; my heart opened. I was beginning to allow myself to love.

My prayers feel like war.
The rumble of explosives,
The quietness of settling dust,

Coexisting
Together in the same breath,
In the same movement,
In the same words.

I feel rest in the tension,
Peace amidst injustice,
Springs of gratitude overflowing
From dry wells of despair.

These are the tears that I cannot cry.

Bearing both laughter and sorrow
Of battles both lost and won.
Like tears,
I fall.

Yet in battle, it is the beating of my breath that remains
a constant prayer in the exhaustion of war.

And perhaps I might find comfort
That these prayers are heard with ease—
For the cries of the innocent echo like gunfire,
The tears of survivors fall like missiles,
And the hearts shattered by bombs
Can expect to be mended with pure gold.

five

NOT A VOICE FOR THE VOICELESS

W HAT IS A NONPROFIT?"
I typed into the Google search.

I had expended my savings to pay for Nekesa, Mara, and Mubanga's tuition for one semester, and I was afraid of what might happen to them next semester. I had an intense desire to see their dreams come into reality, but I knew I couldn't do it alone. Since I've worked with several nonprofits as a filmmaker and photographer, I thought that perhaps with a nonprofit, I could find a way to fully fund their dreams of graduating from university.

I was already moving toward my dream career—working as a documentary filmmaker to spread awareness of the plight of women across the globe. I was going to leverage their stories as a model of hope for us all. But at the same time, I knew it wasn't enough. Creating films did nothing for the people whose stories I captured. *What are you going to do about it?* was the question that troubled me.

Instead of documenting stories as they were, I began to imagine what it might look like to be a part of rewriting their story. What if Mubanga was able to learn in a safe environment outside of the township she was raped in? What if Mara could begin to recognize the power of her voice? What if Nekesa became a social worker to support other survivors of rape? What about the dreams of the countless little girls whose stories I don't yet know? What if their dreams created systemic changes for girls around the world?

I noticed a common thread—lack of access to education made girls more vulnerable to sexual violence. Since education was the prominent desire of the girls I met, perhaps I could begin there.

Their stories birthed a new dream in me. I texted my mom to share my excitement about what I was thinking. I told her that I met these incredible girls and that their dreams compelled me to pay for their school fees from the little savings I had. I told her that I was going to start a nonprofit to support their future education and advocate against sexual violence. She was less than pleased. "I didn't send you to university so that you could throw away your dream! I hope that financial sustainability is within your near future."

Her disapproval devastated me. Yet I understood. Starting a nonprofit was not part of my initial plan nor did it align with cultural expectations of me. She was afraid I was reverting—choosing to go back to the oppression that my family escaped from. What neither of us saw at the time was that my dream was not ending, it was expanding. I was being liberated from the limitations of my own dream, for their dreams were much larger than mine. Their stories would allow others to live freely in hope.

Perhaps Freely in Hope could be the name of this organization. I typed "freelyinhope.org" into the search bar to make sure it wasn't taken.

I wasn't exactly sure how I would bring this hope and freedom to the oppression I witnessed, but perhaps I could try.

When I returned to Kenya the following year for another photography job, Nekesa wanted me to meet her daughter, Hope.

Nekesa and I had just turned twenty-one, our birthdays only days apart. I took a taxi to the Mathare bus stop and saw her standing at the roadside, tall, thin, with short, natural hair and a small baby girl attached to her hip. My heart swelled when I saw her with her baby, who was the embodiment of dreams within her. Hope, now three years old, stared at me intently while Nekesa talked to the driver to give him directions to her house. After engaging in a staring contest with Hope, I lost to look at Nekesa. She was full of energy.

I asked Nekesa if I could film her daily routine, and she agreed. Nekesa rented a small room made of tin in a compound with identical houses stacked closely together. Nothing is private in the slums—everyone knows everyone's business due to the close proximity of the spaces they share. Her walls were covered with pieces of kitenge to create a bit of insulation.

"One day, I am going to build my mom a big, big house in the village and stay with her. Then we can grow our own food," she proudly stated.

She began to peel and chop potatoes into bite-sized pieces for her baby girl. She lit her jiko, balancing the sufuria carefully on the few coals of charcoal left. As the water began to boil, Hope played outside with a football made of rolled-up plastic bags. Nekesa leaned in and out from her door to keep an eye on her. "I usually only eat one meal a day so that my baby can have two," she said with calm assurance as she stirred the boiling bits of potatoes.

Since there wasn't enough space to sit inside, I set up my camera outside to film the interview there. I placed Nekesa in the shade so that the hot sun would reflect off the dirt—casting a warm glow on her body. She sat on a tree stump converted into a stool, balancing her weight and looking around nervously.

I began, "Can you introduce yourself?"

She smiled as she began. "I am a mother, a survivor, and an aspiring social worker. My life has been covered with many, many challenges. Even though I had a daughter from rape, I love her so, so much. Whenever I see her, she is not a reminder of the man who raped me at all. She is only a blessing to me."

Hope ran into the frame and Nekesa picked her up with joy. Her eyes invited her daughter into acceptance, into love, into hope of all the things that could be.

"I am no longer a victim, but a survivor." She continued with Hope on her lap, "My dream is to help other girls see this within themselves—that's why I want to study social work. I want to help survivors know that they are no longer victims too. I want them to see me and say, 'If she can make it, then I can also make it.'" Her eyes welled up.

"Telling your story is the first step to healing," I reassured her.

That day I stopped using the word *victim*. Nekesa taught me that though survivors may have been victimized, their circumstances do not define them. I realized I needed to refute the abusive labels that perpetrators had placed on her by calling into existence the hope that I saw in her—no longer as a victim but as a survivor.

As I had to be careful in the construction of my words, I also had to be careful of how my presence was perceived by others. Little did I know that in this small compound, neighbors were peering curiously out of their windows, staring at me with my camera. I was the first mzungu, the first foreigner, to enter into their space. I did not know how dangerous that would be.

Shortly after I left, neighbors began to knock on her door demanding that she share what the mzungu had given her. She explained that I left her with nothing, only unga flour for the baby. Her neighbors continued to bother her, demanding money she didn't have. She was forced to move for the safety of her and her child.

◆ � ◆

After visiting Nekesa in Mathare, I visited Mara in Kibera. She was busy trying to navigate between her own dreams and the dire needs of her family. She put her own dreams behind her in order to fight for her family's survival. Her brother unexpectedly died from HIV/AIDS, which left his daughter parentless, and she came to stay with Mara. Now Mara had two nieces to feed.

Since Mara recently had graduated from high school, we planned to discuss options for university and what her next steps might be. Before coming, I asked if I could film her story. She agreed, with the condition that her story would share the truth of what's happening in the slums of Nairobi. I reassured her that it would.

I brought Mara's family two large bags of groceries from Nakumatt Supermarket filled with unga flour, sugar, tea leaves, milk, bar soap, cooking oil, white bread, and Blue Band margarine. I bought a few extra things for Mara's nieces: pencils, notebooks, juice, cookies, peanut butter, and strawberry jam.

When I arrived in their home, it looked exactly the same as my previous visit. But Mara was completely different. She was actually talking to me but without eye contact. It was tremendous progress. Mara put on makeup that day, knowing that I was coming to film. A strip of kitenge crowned her head to pull back her natural hair. Charity, Mara's older niece, was sitting at the coffee table finishing her homework with a pencil stub in hand.

"How are you, Charity?" I said, extending my hand.

"I'm fine, how are you?" she responded, shaking my hand.

Mara told Charity to go outside and play.

"To be honest, I lost all hope," Mara said. "When my brother died, I was devastated. I face obstacle after obstacle, and it seems to never end. From school fees for my nieces, medication for my mom, food for all of us, money to bury my brother—going to university seems like an impossible dream." Her face was lit by the glow of a single, naked bulb that dangled by a frayed cord from the ceiling.

"I'm so sorry for your loss," I said as I reached over to touch her elbow. She flinched before I could reach her. I pulled back to set up my camera and started to film.

With a whisper, she told me that she was fighting—fighting against pressures that no teenager should ever face. She told me about the lack of access to clean, running water, which forced her to use a public toilet where she feared being raped. She told me about the rampant prostitution in the slums—how schoolgirls as young as six sell their small bodies for a packet of unga.

"Charity!" She called out the door. The levels on my microphone peaked.

"Yes, Auntie?"

Mara was just making sure she was safe.

"What is it like living in the slums?" I asked.

"It's hard. People here—especially girls—do things like sell their bodies just to get something to eat. It's the only way they can feed their families," Mara's voice lowered again.

"Have they pressured you?" I said.

"All the time, but I can never do that," she said. "I would rather die."

Mara looked down at her thighs pressed tightly together. Her feet bounced up and down, and her eyes darted around the room restlessly, as if she were trying to divert my attention away from her and into her reality.

"How else do you survive?" I asked.

She chuckled and rolled her eyes at my naiveté. "I wash laundry for people, clean houses—you know, the normal things," she said. "I sell vegetables with my mom."

Then she sighed abruptly, and that was my cue to end the invasive questioning.

"What is your dream?" I asked.

She finally looked back at me and concisely said, "My dream is for all my friends who are doing sex work to earn a living. I'd like to see them transformed. I'd like to see them come out of the streets and make something new out of their lives. I'd like to see myself become a woman of impact. I'd like to see a day where I will be able to transform people's lives. My dream is to work in the media as a journalist to expose the truth of how life in the slums unfairly forces women into prostitution." This was the most emotive I had ever seen her. I had what I needed.

"I think journalism is perfect for you," I said as I packed up my equipment. Mara looked inside the shopping bags from Nakumatt. "Oh, asante! The girls will be so happy to see that there is food for them tomorrow. I have never been able to afford snacks for them at school. And I love peanut butter. I don't want the strawberry jam though," she handed it back to me.

"Keep it for the girls," I said.

"No!" she said abruptly as she scrunched up her face, "I can't have it in my house." A bit offended, I took it back.

Catching the 32 bus back to town, I interrogated myself with questions about the safety of young women living in the slums. What would I do if I had to choose between using my savings for school tuition or a meal for my hungry family? How far would I go to ensure the safety of my nieces? What would I do to put uniforms on their backs and keep the lightbulb on for them to study? These were all questions I never had to consider when I was a teenager.

I exhausted myself with constant questioning but found no answers. I wanted so desperately to fix the rampant violence in the slums and take Mara out of her situation, but I also knew that it was not that simple. Otherwise, the masses of aid workers working in Kibera would have done so already.

As I played my footage back that night, I saw the light beaming from Mara's eyes as she spoke about her dreams. I was entranced at the sound of her voice. The first time we met, she wouldn't say a word, but in the interview that day, I could feel her heart hidden behind her words: her grief, her fear, her passion, her love for her nieces. The longer I listened, the more I realized that the solutions would come not from me but from the hope held within Mara's dreams. This dream of becoming a journalist would uncover the truth, and the answers would emerge from her voice and the voices she gathered.

As a filmmaker, I sometimes try so hard to be a voice for the voiceless that I forget that they already have a voice; I'm just not listening.

Instead of empowering, I dehumanize.

Instead of uplifting, I oppress.

Instead of honoring, I forget to see what is beautiful in others.

The closer I listened, the more I recognized the power in her voice, the strength in her stance, and the fire in her eyes.

I was excited to see how Mara's voice might echo beyond Kibera.

*May you realize that you
hold all light within—
remember, more often,
to feel its warmth.*

six

EDUCATION IS NOT THE KEY

AFTER FINISHING MY PHO-
TOGRAPHY job in Kenya, I came back to Richmond to incor-
porate Freely in Hope as a nonprofit organization. I raised enough
funds to pay for next semester's tuition fees for Mara, Nekesa, and
Mubanga. Members of the Kenyan board of directors volunteered
to distribute tuition funds and follow up with the girls when I
was away. We called the survivors "scholars," to counter what they
were called elsewhere. I concurrently produced films for other
international organizations to make ends meet both for myself
and for Freely in Hope.

My film work didn't take me to Zambia, so Mubanga and I
communicated by phone and text when possible. She started to
call me "Mom," which overwhelmed my heart with both honor
and responsibility.

Mubanga was now fifteen. I coordinated with Mubanga's
mom to help her move to a high-performing boarding school
outside of the township. We thought that would be safer, as the
men who raped her were still roaming around Chilanga. No ar-
rests were ever made because the police were still waiting for a
second reported incident.

At her new boarding school, Mubanga was allowed to receive
one five-minute phone call after prayers at noon. I would peri-
odically wake up at 3 a.m. to talk to her, checking in on her
progress and growth. Her grades improved, as did her eloquence

with words. Her texts were written in endearing pidgin: "U cam 2 Lusaka & bcam many girls frnd nt only did u put a smile on de girls face bt oso on de family face. am glad am 1 of dem."

Her writing quickly evolved, and she wrote letters to little girls who grew up in townships like she did:

> There are girls who face life in its sweetness but for others it's as if a storm struck the day they were born. In the townships, life for many girls turn into a struggle to survive. Rape, early pregnancies, and primary school drop-outs are common in our township, but a time has come where we must empower girls. Even though the dark cloud that hangs over the townships has refused to go, know that there is light at the end of the road. God has given us strength to strive, to fight, to use our talents. With it, we can either destroy ourselves or build ourselves toward our future.

While studying, she discovered her dream and shared it with me through text: "My dream is to be doctor so that I can be an example to other girls and show them that women can be influential and save lives. We don't have to stay at home to serve men—we can be outstanding in any occupation we choose."

I saw how, within just a year, education in a safe space expanded her worldview. She graduated high school with high marks, receiving distinctions in the sciences. But when she came home, her new worldview was challenged. The weight of her family's needs—food on the table, school fees for her younger sister, transportation for her mother to get to work—was placed on her. Her mother couldn't wait for her to find a high-paying job and contribute to the communal table that was ever expanding beyond her family of five.

Being back in Chilanga brought about other challenges too—it was a place of traumatic memory, of rape, of attempted suicide, of silencing. She felt like she couldn't get her head above water and was treading in unmet familial expectations and the possibility of re-abuse. Everything at home was a trigger—the kitchen knives, the mango trees, the gate of her old school. She responded by shutting herself in, which led to emotional outbursts. She did this to protect herself—girls her age were becoming mothers to their second child, while the fathers escaped shame. Many of her friends were forced to stay home in their pregnancy, ending the dream of achieving anything higher than an eighth-grade education.

As she moved toward her dreams, she felt alone and misunderstood by those around her. Over the phone she told me that she longed to speak to someone in her language to help her bridge the Tonga culture of her mother, the Bemba culture of her father, the limited mindset of her peers, and the culture she was creating for herself. I listened helplessly as she shared how familiar thoughts of suicide began to creep their way back in. The pain that felt like a knife in her abdomen returned. This was beyond me. My very limited cultural understanding communicated over sporadic phone calls could not suffice.

Now in our third year, Freely in Hope had grown to support ten girls from both urban and rural parts of Kenya. Mara started studying journalism at one of the top private schools in Nairobi. When I gave her the check for her tuition, she bit her lip to conceal her smile. She had been waiting for this opportunity for over a year, begging me for the chance to go to university because she was "just sitting at home." It took me a year to raise money for her tuition in addition to the fees for the other scholars.

I enrolled Mara at her dream university by faith, praying that I could raise enough money to see her graduate. I wanted her to have access to the very best.

I also had faith that she would be able to thrive in a competitive academic environment. She received an average C on the high school standardized exam and with that grade had to pass a year of core courses before being accepted into the journalism program. She was still conversing minimally with me; it was difficult for her to express herself verbally, so she sent me emails instead.

Over email, Mara once asked me for transport money, prefacing it with, "It's really hard for me to ask for something that I cannot get myself." I declined because the local board made it very clear that as an organization that funds scholarships, we could only provide tuition fees, while the scholar's family was responsible for the rest. I was pained at this decision, knowing how much Mara struggled to provide for children that were not her own. I brought Mara's email to the board, advocating for the expansion of services we provided, but we were not receiving enough financially. I didn't know it at the time, but Mara walked to school often from her home deep inside Kibera. For over an hour, she would walk in the heat of the sun and join the hundreds of others commuting to town by foot. She was forced to skip class on days that she had unbearable period cramps. What little money she earned from washing and cleaning went to more important things, like unga for dinner. The suffering of walking in the blinding-hot sun was trivial in comparison to the suffering of seeing her nieces go hungry.

As Nekesa was finishing up her degree in social work, Hope began attending preschool. One day when Nekesa came to pick up Hope from her class, the teacher said to her, "A man came to pick up Hope, saying that he is the father. Since we have never seen him before, we didn't release her." Nekesa was stunned. She hadn't heard from the man who raped her since she was eighteen. Nekesa took Hope and rushed home to find the man standing at her door. He grabbed her and slapped her across the face. He tried to kick the door of her house open, rattling the informal structure of tin and wood. "I'm going to rape you again, and this time, I will give you the disease." He was speaking of HIV. Nekesa screamed as loud as she could, and her neighbor, whom she considered an uncle, came and fought the man off. As he ran away, he shouted, "Next time, I'm going to take your daughter from you, and as for you, I'll slash you with a machete."

Nekesa had no place to go, no place she could find protection, no place to call home. She couldn't go to her village because of threats from her father. She couldn't stay in her current place because of threats from the rapist. So she moved again to protect Hope.

◆ �֎ ◆

"Education is the key to success." I saw this motto handpainted on the cement walls of schools across Kenya and Zambia. Yet I quickly learned that education is only one of the keys.

While school fees were paid, Mubanga's memory of trauma returned together with suicidal thoughts.

While school fees were paid, Mara did not have bus fare to attend class nor money to put food on the table for her nieces.

While school fees were paid, Nekesa was living in fear, attempting to protect her daughter from the rapist who threatened their lives.

The benefits of education were limited. The girls could not thrive academically if their safety was at risk. We needed to expand our funding beyond tuition fees to strengthen their journey toward healing. Counseling, a competitive academic environment, transportation, health care, and safe living conditions were all components of a larger system we were creating. We believed a holistic approach in supporting survivors of sexual violence provided both external protection and internal healing.

I had recently met a Zambian counselor who was just beginning her practice. She worked with Mubanga and her family to help bridge language, culture, expectations, and dreams. In addition to providing all scholars access to counseling in Kenya, we also provided a transportation stipend. We had all scholars checked at a hospital for trauma-induced illnesses like irritable bowel syndrome and wounds resulting from sexual trauma that required antibiotics for sexually transmitted diseases or corrective surgery. We looked into safer housing options for the scholars who didn't have families or were living in close proximity to the abuser.

As the scholars grew academically, they also grew more vocal by expressing their opinions and processing their stories. Nekesa began to share her story with other survivors in Freely in Hope. "I love sharing my story," she told me. "I believe that it will give hope to people who have experienced rape, like me." I was overwhelmed that she would be so bold to share her story on public platforms. I knew that she would change so many hearts, just as she had changed mine.

I was asked to speak at a forum on gender-based violence in Nairobi, and I brought Nekesa along to share the survivor perspective. After explaining Freely in Hope's programs, I invited Nekesa to speak. "Baby girl, you got this," I whispered to her as she came on stage.

> After I was raped, I was so broken. At the same time, I knew that there were so many other women who were in the same situation as me. They were afraid to speak about it, and that is why I wanted to go to university to study social work. I needed to learn how to heal for myself so that I could help other women speak out against sexual violence. As I shared my dream of helping other survivors, Freely in Hope supported my academic dream. My prayer was that one day, I will have a chance to give hope to other women. And I feel like I'm doing just that. I love being a part of Freely in Hope because I see our scholars regain hope after

brokenness. Through their stories, I experienced healing in my own life—this is why we must continue to share our stories to give hope to each other. I know that I am not worthless, I'm no longer ashamed, I'm no longer broken, but I have healed to heal others. For the survivors in the room, please speak out and share your stories. Shake off the dirt, step on it, and let it become a higher stepping stone to help you reach your dreams.

The audience rose to applause. My eyes welled up as I stood to join them. The golden sunlight beamed through the window, touching her natural hair to create a perfect halo.

"Telling your story is the first step to healing," she concluded.

There are wounds that you will never see.

Some have turned into scars,
others have disappeared into the night.

But most invisible wounds remain there—
until the wounded one gathers enough courage
to shed light into the darkness consuming the soul.

This is where healing can begin.

Uniting wounded hearts
are stories in search of healing

And because I first saw your scars
I began to imagine that maybe,

Healing is available to us all.

And as I allowed the stories
of healing to enter my wounded heart,
I saw it within myself—
a different formation,
a transformation, a realization that

Scars are evidence that wounds do heal.

And there I understood
that you cannot give what you do not have.

For to bring healing to others,
you must first attain it yourself.

seven

PLAYING THE ROLE

MARA ARRIVED HUFFING and puffing, having hustled on foot from her nieces' school to meet me at the matatu stage in Kibera. She smiled freely, not hiding her newfound joy. She had pleaded with the principal to let her nieces remain in class for that week, even though exam fees were in arrears. The principal agreed to keep Mara's nieces in school if she could pay the balance in full by Monday—just five thousand shillings ($50.00).

"This weekend, I need to find some small jobs to do," Mara said, explaining her plan to earn the money. "I hate it when my nieces aren't in school. It's not safe for them to stay at home. I'll need to wash clothes for people in the richer parts of town. I never want to make money the way I used to in high school."

Only three years had passed since we first met, and I was seeing her personality unfold more each visit. We sat on her couch, draped with freshly bleached white doilies. Her journalism books were opened on the coffee table where she read by the kerosene lamp.

"Can I make you chai?"

"No, you don't have to," I responded, knowing milk was a luxury.

"I have to make you something if you're in my house!" she said with a smile.

She lit the jiko and placed a small sufuria on top. She sprinkled tea leaves and Mumias sugar into a mixture of water and a generous portion of milk. We watched it to come to a hot boil.

"What's been going on since I saw you last year? What's your highlight?" I asked.

"I have two highlights! One was starting at the university, and guess what? I finished my first semester top of my class!"

"Wow, congratulations! That is so huge considering you didn't even know what you wanted to study at first."

"Imagine! The other highlight was getting a chance to act in my friend's student project for his film class. I love acting. I played the role of a prostitute—I really identified with this character because that used to be me."

I swallowed hard as if eating boiled cassava without chai. I looked at her with an expression of both surprise and concern.

She seemed to have surprised herself too. "I've been wanting to tell you, but I didn't trust you. I was afraid that you would take away my scholarship if you knew, but I've been dying holding on to this secret."

She poured chai for me into a tin cup. "You're going to need this; it's a long story!" It was the first time she spoke freely without my having to interrogate her with questions.

When she was thirteen, one of her friends invited her to a nearby nightclub to escape the pressures of slum life. She had given up on her dream of continuing to high school—there was no money for fees. Her favorite brother, who helped bring income to the family, disappeared without a trace. Her other brother was a drug addict and abandoned his baby at her home. Raising a baby that was not her own and tending to her mother's health, she felt a need for escape.

She went to the club with her friend and danced the night away. A man brought her drinks, she drank, and she lost consciousness. When she woke up, she was lying on the floor, covered in blood. The same man who bought the drinks came in asking, "Why are you still here? Get out!" He threw her on the street. He had paid for her time. The friend that brought Mara to the club had pimped her out—she was paid to find him a virgin.

She walked home silently, slowly, painfully. The streets were busy with people walking on their morning commute. Tears fell down the front of her jean dress while blood was smeared on the back. Her bloodshot eyes lifted to cry for help, but people only looked back in disgust. She said this shameful walk home, alone and neglected, was one of the most difficult moments in her life.

Afraid of her mother finding out that she was at a nightclub, let alone that she had been raped, Mara didn't tell anyone. Weeks later, pregnant and hoping to conceal the memory of the rape, she had an abortion. She remembered the pain vividly—lying on a splintering wooden table as a man used sharp metal scissors to drain life out of her womb. She screamed in pain, thinking she had died, but her body rose up off the wooden table.

Soon she became ill with intense stomach pains and constant vomiting. She returned to the clinic only to learn that she had been carrying twins. Though one had been aborted successfully, the other was still there, dead in her womb.

"This is the story behind my disgust of strawberry jam. The abortion process looked just like that."

If there was any comfort, it was that her mother did not know her pain. Mara had to be the strong one, providing for her mother's medication to ensure her health. She didn't have time to focus on her own health.

It was also a time of political upheaval in Kenya. Young men marched in gangs, chanting fighting songs in their native tongue. Families were glued to their televisions, watching the violence ensue outside of their thin iron sheet walls. Police trolled the roads, pummeling bullets through rioters and innocent by-standers. While coming home after a long day's work of cleaning houses, Mara witnessed a beheading. She ran through the smoke of tear gas and burning cars to a nearby friend's house for safety. When night fell, she decided to spend the night, which she often did since it was overcrowded in her single-roomed home. She also didn't want to risk confronting a machete lest her head be next.

The night became quiet, unusually quiet. Even the irritating buzz of mosquitos had disappeared. Mara tossed and turned—her body still throbbed in pain from the abortion. Suddenly—bang! A gun shot. A woman screamed. Mara and her friend jumped up, afraid to make a sound. Bang! Their door flew open. Three large men wearing police uniforms forced their way in. They carried machetes in their hands and shouted, "If you dare scream, you will die tonight!" Mara and her friend kept their mouths shut while the police raided the tiny room.

"Huku hakuna kitu labda tuji bambe tu," one man said. There is nothing in this house; the only thing we can do is to have fun.

The policemen began to remove their belts. Mara knew this scene all too well. But this time, she was awake to fight back. Fueled by a rush of revenge, she pushed the policeman who tried to pin her down. He attempted to swipe his machete across her face, but Mara blocked it with her arm. Blood ran from her middle finger to her elbow. She didn't want to die from this; her niece was relying on her at home. Mara and her friend were gang raped in turn. All she could do was whisper, "Stop, please stop" as they penetrated her body over and over again.

"I died that day," Mara said. A different Mara was born—one who didn't give shit about life because life only gave shit in return. Body pried opened and violated, anger and bitterness pervaded. But while her hope might have died, the hustle continued. Her mom still needed medication, her niece still needed to eat, and school fees still needed to be paid for both of them.

The quickest way to make money in Kibera was through prostitution. Many of her friends had already started their careers at thirteen years old, and so Mara was considered a latecomer at fourteen. Without an option, Mara began working the streets at night, earning between twenty to fifty shillings ($0.20-$0.50) per customer and serving between seven to ten customers per night. Some of them would pay as much as two hundred shillings ($2.00) if she was lucky. But luck is unjust and short-lived. When morning came, she would have to surrender half of her earnings to the pimp, a terrible old woman who thought she owned girls like she owned cows.

With her little earnings, Mara would bring food home for her family in the morning before leaving to attend her high school classes during the day. At night, she would return to the brothel, and the vicious cycle would start all over again. To protect her mom, she told her that she worked the nightshift at a nearby restaurant.

Yet even in the darkness Mara saw a glimmer of hope, however faint, in pursuing her academic dreams. Taking shelter in that tiny ray of hope, she worked the streets to pay for her first three years of high school. I met Mara at this point of her story, drowning in her oversized T-shirt. "I was actually high that day I came to meet you because I was so numb from my work the night before. My mom begged me to come meet you."

Though Mara had her final year of high school fees paid through Freely in Hope, she struggled to support her niece and mom, so she continued to work in the brothel during school holidays. "Some customers even pay not to have sex but to beat you up," Mara recalled. "And one night, a man beat me so badly that my friend had to rescue me. She thought I was being murdered. Bruised and bleeding, I knew I had to get out. That pimp said the most evil things to get me to stay. She said that I'd never be worth anything other than sex, that education is only for smart girls, that I deserved to be punished for my sins. Another friend had recently left the brothel, and I thought I should too. I followed in her footsteps and left that life behind me."

But her liberation didn't last long. Mara's mom became ill again. Her niece was chased from school for not paying fees. Her favorite brother was finally found—dead from HIV/AIDS—and his daughter was left at her doorstep. She now had two children to feed. So she went back to the brothel, and the pimp scoffed at her failure, "Heh! Mara thinks she can live without me. I'm the hand who feeds you all! You will never make it without me!"

"She was a terrible woman who wanted nothing more than to make our lives more miserable than the misery she faced in her past life," Mara stated.

Work continued as usual until Mara started her journalism program in university. Living in what seemed like an impossible dream, she began to imagine something new. When she rose to the top of her class at her university, she began to believe that her worth was something beyond her body.

Surprised at her own success, she decided to leave the brothel for good. She found hope in pursuing her academic dreams so that she could tell the unheard stories of her friends still caught in the vicious cycle of prostitution. She got off drugs on her own and had been clean for three months. "And that is how I left!" she said, grinning from ear to ear.

We had been talking for hours, and it was now dark. Mara screwed the lightbulb into the dangling cord above. "You didn't finish your chai," she noticed. I had been immersed in the saga of her story. I downed the cold chai and rummaged through my pocket. I realized I only had a ten-shilling coin on me.

"Take KBS, the blue bus. It's much safer and won't have pickpockets on there," she said as she handed me a twenty-shilling coin. It was just enough to get home.

Forgive yourself

for not knowing
what you know now.

For this will expand the heart's
capacity for compassion

for self

and

for others

who do not yet know
what they will.

eight

CINEMATIC IMAGINATION

Bᴇɴᴛ ᴏᴠᴇʀ ʙᴜᴄᴋᴇᴛs ᴏꜰ soapy water, I scrubbed remnants of dirt out of my pants. Breathing hard, hands aching, fighting back tears—the task of scrubbing my dirty clothes made me identify with a pain I had never before experienced. Hand washing laundry is one of many things I never have had to do on a regular basis, but it isn't the only thing.

Mara's story haunted me. My cinematic imagination reeled through her story in my mind. I saw her alone in the underground clinic awaiting an abortion, surrounded by policemen on top of her as her arm dripped with blood, trapped in a closet-sized brothel, beaten and bloodied on the concrete floor. I keeled over from a heavy heart and wept.

I stopped scrubbing to allow my hands to rest and heart to feel. I played the footage of her interview that I filmed a year before. I noticed when she was talking about the issues surrounding the poverty of Kibera, she wouldn't dare look at me as she told me how girls as young as six sell their small bodies for a packet of unga.

"How else do you survive?" I ignorantly asked.

"I wash laundry for people, clean people's houses—you know, the normal things," she said.

I replayed the interview again, and I began to see nuances that I hadn't seen before: her defensive stance, her lack of eye contact, her bloodshot eyes, her anxiety in every uneven exhale. She was speaking to me in code—washing laundry and cleaning houses wasn't the only work she was doing to survive. Selling sex on the streets to buy unga and a high school education shouldn't be considered normal. I flashed back to when I reached out to touch her elbow after hearing her brother died; she flinched before I even touched her. I could not see it then, but she was adamantly reaching back—desperate to be pulled out of the hell she was in. Her body was telling me pieces of her story that I was blind to.

So much had changed since that invasive interview; now Mara was able to use her voice to tell her own story. Still, the feeling of failure followed me.

I grit my teeth to wring out as much water as I could from my clothes. I hung them up to dry. With each peg that I placed on the drying line, I remembered email after email telling me that she could not bear the thought of sitting at home with nothing to do. After graduating from high school, she would have to wait for a year until her high school results came out. Then, she could enroll in university. She was deathly afraid of this yearlong waiting period—afraid of being left without the prospect of school, without the possibility of escape, that I would forget and never come back again. She reminded me of this fear persistently, asking when I would return. I now began to understand why— she was desperate to escape the confines of the brothel. Some of the emails were left unanswered because I did not understand the reason behind her sense of urgency.

My mind's eye saw the fragments of her story finally piece together along the timeline, and I felt myself suffocating under the weight of sopping wet clothes. I went to the market to get some mangoes and fresh air.

Two little girls held hands at the roadside. "How are you?" they called out in synchronized voices. Images of Mara's nieces came into focus. For a teenager, I noticed that Mara was extremely responsible, motherly, and protective over them since they were in her care. I was often startled with how quickly her voice would fluctuate from soft and timid with me to booming and authoritative toward her nieces. She loved them as if they were her own, the ones she could not give birth to. I recalled her telling me that a small girl was raped within her compound. The rapist tricked her into his home with candy. Men, relatives of the small girl, beat the rapist up and killed him. She told me she's taught her nieces how to scream if anyone were to touch them. I remembered filming her nieces jumping rope together in this same compound, unaware of the dangers lurking behind tin walls.

I passed by Nakumatt Supermarket, where I buy her family food for my visits. On one of the visits, Mara took everything except the strawberry jam. Offended that she didn't accept my gift, I left in a haste to start editing her interview footage. I didn't notice the look on her face when she saw the glass jar of red jelly—her eyes began to water from repulsion. She gave it back to me with one hand while placing her other hand on her belly.

Walking home with my bag full of mangoes, I imagined how humiliated and betrayed she felt while she walked home after being raped at thirteen. I remember walking that same pathway while filming her. She kept her eyes to the ground and sighed as if silently praying that I would sense her discomfort of reliving a memory she would rather forget.

I blamed myself for missing her cues. Most of the time, I did not know how to respond, for her encrypted messages were too numerous to piece together. I didn't have solutions to protect her from the insecurities of living in Kibera. I didn't have the funds for the university education she desperately wanted at the time that she needed it. I didn't know that she was fighting to preserve her life, fighting for her academic dreams, fighting to care for her family in all the ways she knew how.

Not knowing of the hell she was living in, I felt like I had failed her. Every time I visited, I was just trying to get the shot. I hated myself for it.

For it is in times of uncertainty,
that hope becomes a practice.

It is in times of loss,
that our ability to hold hope is strengthened.

It is in times of suffering,
that our capacity to hope is expanded.

nine

LUSAKA HEAT

I CARRIED MARA'S STORY and self-blame with me to Zambia. I finally got a photography job there, and I stayed with Mubanga's family. Mubanga met me at the airport. Her natural hair was slicked back with Vaseline, and her eyes were lined in black. Three years had passed since we saw each other last. She was now a maturing seventeen-year-old.

We glided through the business district of Lusaka, bouncing along unpaved dirt roads toward Chilanga. Arriving at her home, I was ecstatic to see her family again. They embraced me with dancing and singing. I played outside in the dirt with Mapalo, the youngest sister, while Grace, the oldest sister, danced as she swept the house. I loved being in their home because it was full—full of laughter and dancing, singing and pure joy.

After catching up with Mubanga's mom, I came to the bedroom and found Mubanga lying there alone. The curtains were drawn. Though our relationship was held together by delayed phone calls at intermittent timeframes across the sea, I noticed that something had changed. She seemed estranged. Numb. Distant. Unlike the sassy girl I knew on the phone. For her, there was no laughter, no dancing, no conversations typical of a playful teenager. She had just completed her first semester at the medical university—her dream school. I thought she would be more excited than exhausted. Only communicating by phone over the last three years, I realized that I couldn't see the sadness in her eyes.

I sat with Mubanga's parents as the girls prepared dinner. The kitchen was blasting with the sounds of Afrobeats and popping oil. Smoke from the mbaula wafted into the house as Grace fanned the embers, frying kapenta, dried sardines, over the hot coals. Mapalo sat on the floor grating fresh tomatoes to make a salty sauce. Mubanga stirred nshima in a large aluminum pot with her whole body.

With a chitenge tied around her waist, Mubanga came to the sitting room with a pitcher of warm water in one hand and a basin at her hip. She knelt to the floor and poured the warm water over my dusty hands. Mapalo ran in from the shop and placed a new bottle of water on the table just for me. After serving us, the girls ate on the kitchen floor with each other. Their sisterly banter continued behind closed doors.

As I ate with Mubanga's parents, I could see their pride in their daughter, as she was the first in their family to enroll in university. Mubanga's mom had always believed that if her daughters could succeed academically, then she would have raised them to be better than her. Filled with high hopes that Mubanga would become a doctor, we celebrated the feeling of success that arose in each of us.

Mubanga warmed water for me on the remaining hot coals in the mbaula outside. Water is precious here in Chilanga—the girls collect buckets of water every morning at dawn. She came to me, kneeled and said, "Mom, your water is ready." Dumping the warmed water over my head felt like a divine cleansing after traveling for over thirty-five hours.

I woke up in the middle of the night and noticed that the television was still on, its blue light flickering against the hallway walls. I got up to turn it off but found Mubanga sitting there alone. She was staring blankly into the television. I flipped the lights on and startled her.

"I'm sorry, I didn't mean to scare you," I said.

"I can't sleep."

"What's going on?"

"Nothing."

I sat with her while my heavy eyes drifted in and out of sleep.

She exhaled abruptly and said, "Remember I told you about my friend from school, Keyon?"

"Yes."

"I lent my Bible to him. He knows I am a Christian and said he was interested in learning more about Christianity."

He asked her to come to his house to pick up the Bible. He poured her some juice—it was mango juice, her favorite—and told her the interesting things he learned in this newfound book. Before Mubanga could finish her juice, the room began to spin, and she passed out. When she woke up, she was naked on Keyon's bed. Unaware of what had happened to her, she was still in a daze, in pain, and nauseous. Keyon said, "It says here in your Bible that 'two shall become one,' so we are 'one' now, right?" It was late at night, and she had no way of getting home safely. He continued to rape her throughout the night as she drifted in and out of consciousness.

I stared at her intently, trying to listen, but all I could hear was the pounding of my heart. For the first time, I saw her cry.

I was burning with fury and interrogated her with questions about where Keyon lived so that I could visit him with a machete. She said that he graduated and went to London. She didn't report it because she knew nothing would happen. The laws of justice were not on her side—she would only be accused for going to his house in the first place. "What do you mean you didn't report?" My voice raised into a loud whisper. Anger welled within my body, and I started to rise. She grabbed my hands to anchor me down and said, "Let's pray and go to sleep." She prayed over us, but I couldn't hear her prayer; I was angry with the God she prayed to.

◆ �֎ ◆

Mubanga refused to report the rape. She felt as if it were her fault for going there. This was Zambia, after all, where a girl's voice has no value. She argued that the police would ask her if she knew him. Since she did, they would assume he was her boyfriend and therefore did not rape her. She believed the lie, too, blaming herself for all the things that made her a girl.

I was adamant about seeking justice for Mubanga. I felt that I had failed her by being absent in her life in the past three years. I pushed Mubanga hard to seek justice for herself by reminding her that she was worthy of justice. I didn't believe that Zambia's justice system could be so unmoved by a survivor's story, so I dragged her along to meetings, desperately clinging to hope. We sought advice from a lawyer, paid several visits to the police station, met with the government-sanctioned gender-based violence unit, had a session with a counselor, but it seemed that nothing could be done. In Zambia, convicting someone who was out of the country was a nearly impossible feat with no evidence, no hospital record, and late reporting. Mubanga was right.

One day, Mubanga received a text from Keyon. It said: "I'm HIV positive."

Early the next morning, we traveled twenty minutes to a neighboring township where no one knew her to have her tested for HIV. When we walked into the clinic, everything seemed to stop. Everyone—patients and nurses alike—stared at me, a Chinese girl, walking into a township clinic. To protect Mubanga, I asked a nearby nurse, "Auntie, where is the VCT department?" Unconcerned, she pointed to the back of the hospital. We hurried to the back to find the door labeled Voluntary Counseling and Testing. An old man and a young nurse reclined in their seats in their closet-sized office. They looked surprised to see us. I explained the reason for our visit, and the old man asked Mubanga,

"Why are you getting tested?" Mubanga told him that she was drug-raped. "What were you doing at his house then? And anyway, how do you know it was rape?" She rolled her eyes—it was exactly as she anticipated. The young woman drew Mubanga's blood.

Thirty seconds passed. I felt like throwing up. Zambia ranks number seven of countries with the highest rate of HIV. Hearts pounding in tandem, Mubanga squeezed my hand tighter each second. We held our breath. The young woman looked at the white strip and said, "You are negative." We sighed in relief and embraced each other. In that moment, we celebrated—but I found it strange that we were celebrating a negative test. She shouldn't have had to get tested in the first place.

On our way home, Mubanga turned to me and said, "When I told you what happened, I wish that you didn't say anything. I wish that you just gave me a hug." Ashamed, I didn't respond, feeling like I had failed her once again. I was so focused on chasing after justice that I left her behind in the process. Justice was not what she needed at the moment. I was blind to the fact that there are many things that I cannot fix and even more things that I cannot control—like physical illness.

◆ ❋ ◆

I had developed a terrible cough, likely from operating on little sleep and overfunctioning from anger-induced adrenaline. Every day I had scheduled multiple meetings to build partnerships with Freely in Hope, connect with community organizations, organize local speaking gigs, facilitate support groups for survivors of sexual violence, link advocacy initiates for child survivors of rape, and attempt to seek justice for Mubanga's case. I hustled hard, thinking that the more I worked, the higher the chance that we could open a case against Keyon. I was exhausted and enraged.

My cough persisted, but I refused to let it stop me. I had laundry to wash. Mapalo got me a small packet of washing powder from the kiosk next door. She helped me wash my clothes because I was too slow.

◆ ✼ ◆

On a glorious Sunday afternoon, Mubanga and I spoke at a local organization of a dozen young leaders. The director of the hosting organization told me that he brought several girls that he had recently met, including a survivor named Ruby. He pointed to a girl wearing a bright red dress, saying, "She wants to talk to you." Her face wore an expression that was both somber and angry. I tried to greet her, but she wouldn't respond. Arms tightly folded across her thin body, she did not look up, and she refused to participate during group discussions.

"Baby girl, you got this," I told Mubanga before she went up to talk. She shared the story of when she was first raped at thirteen years old and how her trauma resulted in attempted suicide. She facilitated a lively discussion on healing after trauma. The young leaders in the room were thoroughly engaged, sharing their dreams for a violence-free Zambia.

"Your experiences are not written on your body," Mubanga said, seeming to direct her story to Ruby. "I'm telling you my story because I hope that you heal from painful experiences and fight for your dreams. Allow your pain to pour out and make room for your healing."

I snapped photos looking up at Mubanga—I was proud of her confident storytelling and facilitation skills. Even in the aftermath of the recent rape, she was incredibly articulate and courageous. A proud mom, I looked around at the expressions of the young leaders as they interacted with Mubanga's story. I saw Ruby, still with her arms crossed and head down, but her eyes gazed at Mubanga.

◆ ❈ ◆

The next day, I was surprised to receive a call from Ruby. She said that she was moved by Mubanga's story and wanted to talk to me. We met at a cafe where she ordered juice and I listened. Struggling through hyperventilating sobs, she iterated her story for the first time, of growing up in a township rampant with senseless murders, being tricked and raped by a friend, being rejected by her family for being a victim of such a vile crime, being raped a second time after rededicating her life to God, feeling unloved by God, experiencing sporadic paralysis as a result of trauma, being accused of witchcraft by the church, working in prostitution to fund her education, and failing multiple attempts of suicide.

Looking up, she asked me, "How am I supposed to gain my dignity back?"

My body's temperature escalated into a feverish headache. I suddenly became nauseous, my vision blurred. Ruby's face was fuzzy. "Look here," she said. I was trying to refocus on her face. "Look here!" she said again because I wasn't paying attention to the area on her skin she was pointing to. She pointed to a mark on her collarbone. A series of three cuts were scattered across her body—from her collarbone to her stomach, from her forearm to her wrist. "These are scars from the cuts made by the witch doctor my mom called as an attempt to heal my paralysis. The cuts are supposed to release bad blood. My mom said that the reason why I had paralysis was because I am a prostitute—but I'm not a prostitute!" She buried her face into her hands and sobbed.

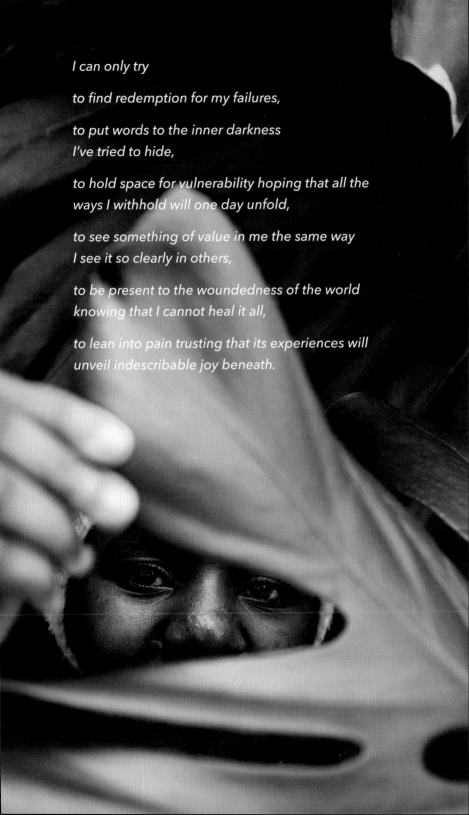

I can only try

to find redemption for my failures,

to put words to the inner darkness
I've tried to hide,

to hold space for vulnerability hoping that all the
ways I withhold will one day unfold,

to see something of value in me the same way
I see it so clearly in others,

to be present to the woundedness of the world
knowing that I cannot heal it all,

to lean into pain trusting that its experiences will
unveil indescribable joy beneath.

ten

LOW COST OR HIGH COST

In THE DESERT HEAT OF Zambia's hot season, I couldn't get out of bed for a week. I was sweating profusely—head pounding, body aching. Because I couldn't come out for meals, Mubanga would bring food to my room: nshima and stewed tomatoes, white bread and a fried egg, a boiled egg, white bread and nothing more. I tried my best to eat as a gesture of gratitude, but I felt guilty because I knew it was all they had. Besides, everything I ate and drank came right back up. My phone was ringing constantly. I struggled to answer a few of the phone calls and scheduled back-to-back interviews the next day.

On my way to the meetings, Mubanga's mom brought me to a local clinic. Thinking I had malaria, the clinic prescribed me hydroxychloroquine, which I was to take three times per day. I went straight to my meetings. As I attempted to conduct the interviews, I tried to scribble down their answers but I could not control my body's mobility.

That night, I vomited water constantly throughout the night. As soon as I would swallow the malaria pill, it would come right back up. Eventually I passed out from dehydration.

In the morning, I had nothing left—no words to say, no power to make decisions, no strength to move. I told Mubanga to pack my bag for me as I watched helplessly. She folded my clothes and placed them neatly in my suitcase. Seeing my condition, she asked, "Are you sure you want to leave today? Why don't we go to the hospital instead." I refused. She tried to help me get up to change my sweaty clothes, but I collapsed to the floor.

Seeing that I could barely stand to dress myself, I finally set aside my pride and called my mom. It was 4 a.m. in California. "Hi, Mom? Not to alarm you, but I've had a terrible fever and headache for a week. I haven't been able to eat and I've been vomiting water. My flight leaves in a few hours and my taxi is here. What should I do?"

Without hesitation my mom firmly replied, "Either you rest now or you rest forever."

We took the taxi to the hospital instead of the airport. At the hospital, I slumped over in my chair, mumbling yes and no to the questions they asked. The nurse drew my blood and told me that I did not have malaria. I felt myself passing out again. Noticing that I was barely conscious, the nurse gave me a painkiller shot on my butt cheek. They rushed me to another hospital and hooked me up to an IV drip. Since Mubanga was at school, her sister Grace stayed with me the whole day. Every time I moved, she came over to ensure I was still alive. When she heard me moaning in pain, she asked the nurses to give me more pain-killers, and finally, I was able to rest. When I woke up from my pounding in my head, Grace was still there beside me.

Connected to an IV drip, I slept the whole night for the first time in several weeks. When I woke up, the doctor asked, "How do you feel?"

"A little better."

"Then you can go home."

"I don't feel well enough to go home."

"Then you can stay."

Confused, I tried to ask what the diagnosis was. The pain in my body had decreased as well as my fever, but I was afraid of going anywhere without being fully healed—or at least aware of what illness I had. The doctor's lack of concern frustrated me, but I didn't have the mental capacity to articulate how I felt nor the physical energy to advocate for myself. When Mubanga came to visit after school, I told her to get me out of there. She took my wallet to pay my bill and we went to the University Teaching Hospital.

When we arrived, Mubanga and Grace lifted my arms around their necks and dragged me to the overcrowded waiting area outside. I was surrounded by people, sitting on the floor, lying on their chitenge, crying, sweating, moaning, trying to hold on, just like me. I felt united in our common pain.

The hospital wing was stacked with hospital beds. Some had two people on one bed. Nurses and doctors scurried back and forth holding pans of bodily waste, used syringes, and white tablets. The windows and doors were wide open to let the nominal breeze air out the suffocating smell. The eyes of the conscious patients followed me, and an overwhelming feeling of shame came over me.

I was leaving what was considered the "low-cost" wing to get to the "high-cost" wing on the other side. Passing through white double doors, I felt like I was in another hospital world. The massive room was lit not by sunlight but by a fluorescent green light. The air conditioning was on full blast. There were rows and rows of empty seats. I sat in the seat closest to me, clinging to the armrest as if holding onto whatever dignity I had left. It cost twenty dollars to be seen by the high-cost doctor. Mubanga sat across from me with a look of helpless concern. I felt ashamed that she had to see me like this.

The young doctor looked painfully unpracticed. I told him that I had just come from another hospital and they had no diagnosis for my illness. He said there were a series of tests I needed to figure out what the problem was.

"Have you been tested for HIV?" he asked.

"No, it's not necessary."

"Your problem could be HIV, you need to be tested."

"Look, I know how HIV is transmitted. I do not have HIV."

He was unconvinced and continued to argue with me. Defeated, I dropped my head on his desk and said, "Fine, please just give me a painkiller." I hated how desperate I sounded, but I had to say it before my head exploded. He showed me to a room full of rusty beds and broken wheelchairs. A nurse pulled me behind a curtain where there was another woman sitting on the hospital bed. Her cheeks were sunken and her body gaunt. But her eyes were young and strong. I leaned onto the bed she was sitting on as the nurse injected me in the butt cheek. I winced, and the woman looked back at me with empathetic eyes.

Mubanga dragged me around the hospital so that I could get poked, scanned, and tested. We came back to the waiting area as the doctor prepared my medication. As I sat there waiting, I felt my body temperature rise again, and I became paralyzed. The noises around me escalated to the point where I could only hear ringing in my ears and indistinct sounds overlapping in tangled disarray. The fluorescent green lights started to pulse and penetrate my brain. Strange voices pounded in my head, saying that I was a failure, weak, and unworthy to be alive. I felt my lungs closing in. I jumped out of my seat to break out of paralysis. This became the first of many anxiety attacks.

I ran outside to feel my heart beat life into my body. I sat on the curb and buried my face in my hands, praying to become invisible to the crowds passing by. Mubanga came running after me and sat beside me. After a while she asked, "Mom, are you okay?"

I didn't respond.

"Are you frustrated?"

With my face still in my hands, I nodded, for my voice would crack if I spoke. I was frustrated because I was unable to do anything for myself.

"You would do the same for me. You help me in all the drama I put you through," she said, trying to make me laugh.

"But it's me," I said. It took everything to speak this truth without my body collapsing.

"You deserve to be taken care of too. You're still the same strong mom I know," she kindly replied and wrapped her arms around my heavy shoulders.

To be called strong in that moment made me feel like a fraud. I wanted to slip away from an embrace I did not deserve.

◆ ❋ ◆

The hospital supplied me with tiny yellow antibiotics and said I had an "unknown virus." A friend suggested I move out of the bustling township and into her quiet home. I stayed there to recover from many things unknown to me.

I had overworked myself in an attempt to be strong and to dispel the lie of weakness. I thought that if I only worked harder, if I could only see an end to this injustice, put these rapists in prison, and put all these survivors in school, then I would be strong. I had imprisoned myself in a web of impossible expectations based on my need to control. But physical illness was something that I could not control.

The dreadful antibiotics weakened me. After taking the yellow pill, I would shut my eyes to trick myself into falling asleep. But my mind was wide awake. I shamed myself for being in this sickly state. *How could you run an organization that exists to end sexual violence when sexual violence is perpetuated against your own? If you can't achieve this mission, what are you even doing? If the very thing that we exist to do—to protect our scholars from violence—continues to happen under our care, your presence has no purpose. You have failed the girls that you have grown to love.*

I replayed their stories of trauma in my mind. Mara's story consumed me with grief. Nekesa's story consumed me with fear. Mubanga's story consumed me with anger. Ruby's story consumed me with uncertainty. These stories haunted me night and day, inhibiting my ability to pray. Even if I tried to pray, I didn't feel worthy of being heard. It was difficult for me to believe in the presence of God if God did not intervene for these girls in their innocence. "God, where are you?" became my only plea.

I lay in bed unable to move, sweating, nauseous, and barely conscious. I was unable to rest from the anxiety attacks and tormenting flashbacks. In the night, I often awoke in panic with eyes wide open and darkness staring back at me. In the morning, I would often stare out the window into bright sunlight until my eyes began to water. This forced me to cry, because my sorrow refused to express itself in tears.

Feeling vastly distant from God, my memory returned to the conversation with Mara over chai. I remembered the countless times God had freed her: from self-hatred to an all-embracing love, from drug addiction to sobriety, from the dangers of prostitution to the safety of community, from silencing her dreams to pursuing a university degree, from hopeless despair to a powerful example of liberation.

God, where are you?

God was present throughout the trajectory of her story.

The memory of Mara's liberation gave me the strength to breathe into another day.

In the morning, Mubanga came to visit. Unable to stand, I laid in bed while yelling instructions to her in the kitchen, "Cut the ginger into large slices. Smash the garlic. Wash the chicken with salt. Put everything in the pot with a cup of rice. Fill the pot with water. Turn the stove on low heat." My body needed something familiar, like the taste of my grandfather's jook, to generate some sense of energy in an unfamiliar space. I was familiar with this feeling of pain. But this time, it was tainted with tremendous suffering unfamiliar to me. I did not know how to feel my own emotions.

"Mom! How do you light this mbaula?" Mubanga called from the kitchen.

I was too used to feeling the emotions of others.

*Maybe our greatest fear
is not of being loved,
but of being transformed
by that love.*

eleven

HEALED IN KILLING FIELDS

GOD WAS SILENT IN MY GRIEF,
silent in my anger,
silent in my failure,
silent in my defeat,
silent in my suffering,
silent in their suffering.

After a month of eating jook with my tiny yellow pills, I finally felt strong enough to travel home. It was time to leave, but I didn't want to leave like this. I felt as if I had failed Mubanga, but I knew that staying would not allow me to fully heal. On my way to the airport, I picked up the rest of my things from Mubanga's house in Chilanga. Earlier I had asked her dad to sew a pair of pants for me, to support his business. That day, I tried them on, but they didn't fit. "You lost weight," he said as he checked my measurements again. It was then that I realized that I had. I needed to gain my weight back—and perhaps my dignity as well.

The accumulation of three years filled with stories of unspeakable violence escalated into physical illness. The myth of invincibility forced its way onto my tired shoulders. I carried the weight of their stories as if they were my own, but I wasn't strong enough to carry it all. I didn't think that I deserved to do this work because I couldn't keep the violence from infiltrating our community. I was angry with myself that I couldn't do enough, didn't do enough to shield them from harm, even if it meant risking my health. After hearing story after story of trauma upon trauma that had affected the girls that I love most, I believed that the issues surrounding my community were reflections of my failed leadership.

It fractured my spirit even more than my body.

My body rejected everything, including water, but my spirit rejected my sense of worth.

My head was consumed with relentless pain, but my mind was tortured with thoughts of inadequacy.

I barely had the strength to sit up and didn't think that my strength could stand against injustice any longer.

I lost fifteen pounds and thought that I lost my calling in the process.

I had forgotten what the presence of God felt like.

After I returned to California, I discussed what had happened with my board. They were concerned, noticing how the trauma I experienced caused me to question my purpose. I was in disbelief—ashamed to admit that I was on the verge of giving up. At their guidance, I reluctantly embarked on a three-month sabbatical in search of healing and discernment on whether I had the capacity to continue in my vocation or not. Nekesa had recently graduated with her degree in social work, so I hired her to respond to the scholars' needs, distribute funds, and conduct regular home visits in Kenya. Nekesa was eager to take up this position to prove her sense of responsibility. Now, she could finally begin building the house for her mom in the village. She assured me that she would take care of everything and that she wouldn't disturb me while I was away. As she took on this leadership role, I realized that her position on staff aligned with my dream that Freely in Hope would be led by survivors of sexual violence. I left, trusting that the organization would be in good hands.

◆　❈　◆

When I embarked on my sabbatical, the year was 2014—commemorating twenty years since the genocide in Rwanda. My mentors invited me on a pilgrimage there to journey through places of immense pain and tremendous hope as a means to engage in the pain and hope in our own lives. I was hesitant to go, because I knew I would delve into the hellish reality of a violent massacre. At the same time, I felt that I might find redemption for my pain by learning in a place outside of the context of sexual violence. I thought a new environment would allow me to escape the pain that I secretly harbored within me. Perhaps, by stepping into the pain, I might find the hope I was desperately searching for.

I traveled with eight others. We gathered daily to meditate together, practicing forms of contemplative prayer observed by the saints and mystics of long ago.

During the genocide, churches, which are usually thought of as places of refuge, were targets for mass destruction. As we approached the threshold of a church that morning, I peered through the bullet-pierced doors. Inside was a massive amount of blood-stained clothes hanging lifelessly over pews where they once sat. Ten thousand Tutsis sought refuge at this church, but that day, instead of savoring last moments together, they were praying their lives could end faster.

We walked around the circumference of the church and down to the crypt below. There laid a pure white coffin holding the bones of a young woman who had been gang raped in this church. Her body had been pierced by two spears to resemble a cross. As we remembered her, I also remembered the pain of many of the scholars and how death, often so close, escaped them. I felt like throwing up, feeling strange that stories of rape continued to follow me.

We practiced our first meditation there, surrounded by off-white walls splattered with blood that had dried to brown. I could still hear the screams echo against the walls.

Sitting in a circle with my fellow travelers, I felt very small. Flashbacks consumed my mind—I saw Nekesa shielding her child from the rapist, Mara pinned to the floor by policemen, Mubanga getting tested at the clinic, the woman's face inside the pure white coffin. I couldn't focus, I couldn't listen, I couldn't be present to myself or to those around me. Darting my eyes around the room and shifting my body weight from left to right, I distracted myself from feeling pain. The horrific images cycling through my head impeded my ability to be still. Stillness caused a flood of emotions to wash over me. To fight against it, I became numb.

Our first exercise was to simply breathe. My mentor began, "There's a story of Jesus where a crowd was following him into Jerusalem. At the Jerusalem gate was a poor, blind man who was always there begging. He cried out, 'Jesus, son of David, have mercy on me!' The disciples told the man to be quiet because Jesus was busy with the crowd of people following him. Despite the disciples' reprimand, the blind man cried out again, 'Jesus, son of David, have mercy on me!' Hearing him, Jesus stopped and turned to the blind man. He gently asked, 'What do you need?' The blind man responded, 'I want to see.'"

She continued: "Jesus asked the blind man for his need so that he might recognize his own blindness. It is in this recognition of his deepest need that he was healed."

We practiced breath prayer, in which we breathed a name for God on the inhale and our need at the exhale. I closed my eyes and listened to my heartfelt need: healing. "Jesus, be my healer" was my prayer, but I found it hard to breathe. After a few moments of irregular breathing of this prayer, I felt my chest compress and my heart beat faster. My inhales and exhales became shorter and quicker. I felt the heavy weight of bones on top of me, so I opened my eyes.

Everyone else was still breathing, still praying, still. In my anxiety, I was too afraid to close my eyes again.

The next phase of this prayer was to listen to God's unique name for us and God's response to us. Cautiously I closed my eyes again in an attempt to listen.

Almost instantly, I heard, "Baby girl, you got this."

I opened my eyes in surprise because this was the same phrase that I used to encourage the scholars to lead into their vision. I was stunned, wondering if perhaps I was worthy enough to be seen by God. Even as I failed time and time again, I was not far from God's love. For God's presence was found within my very breath.

Early in the morning, my phone had a series of missed calls. It was Mubanga.

Since Mubanga was raped by Keyon, she was not the same. No matter how many times I told her it was not her fault, I could not make her believe otherwise. She numbed her pain away by making herself fall—hard—hitting her head on the floor, hoping that a smack on the head would end her life.

I quickly called her back and counted each ring, holding my breath until she picked up.

"Mom?" Her voice was like charcoal.

"Yes? Hello? Are you there?"

She was crying on the other end.

"What's going on?"

Between sobs, she struggled to speak, "I just picked up my results from school. I failed. If I have failed my family, my community, then how can I ever make something of my life? I'm tired—tired of fighting, tired of trying, tired of feeling like everything is my fault. My family has all their hopes in me to help my little sister go to school, but if I can't pass my own classes, how can I help her?"

Being the only child on scholarship in her extended family, Mubanga was on a pedestal. Academic success equated approval from the community and honor to her family. To fail this opportunity, to her, was to disappoint other girls who looked up to her.

"Where are you?" I asked.

"I'm at the cemetery. Under the same mango tree where I wish I died when I was first raped. I have a knife in my hand, and I just called to say that I'm sorry for failing you. I'm sorry for failing my parents. I would rather they find a child who's dead than a child who's failed."

Just when I thought I could not hold any more pain, this moment required that I find space. I jumped out of bed. My heart felt like it was racing to meet her where she was—the cemetery that she was raped at when she was thirteen. Where the rapists attempted to hide their sin, she would hide her body.

"You are not a failure. There will be more opportunities for school after this. You are not going to give up. You're going to put the knife down and go home. Now!"

"I can't," she continued to sob.

I turned on my mom voice—the voice, like my mother's, that is so definitive that doing anything else would be a scandalous crime. I hoped that my words could somehow take away the knife so that she could hold my hand instead.

"Baby girl, listen to me. Put. The knife. Down." I held my breath, waiting for her response, praying that my firm words brought consolation instead of shame.

"Okay," Mubanga sighed, pushing all the air out of her lungs.

"Did you drop the knife?"

"Yes."

"Go home, and call me when you get there."

"Okay, Mom."

She hung up the phone. My body was shaking. I went outside and ran through Rwandan soil and past rice fields. I ran in an effort to feel again. During my illness, I had suppressed all feeling to protect myself from harrowing flashbacks, from the inability to maintain control when triggered, from the probability of having my heart grieved again, from engaging in pain that I could not heal. As blood pumped through my veins with every stride, I needed to feel that I had something of warmth to offer to this cold world.

In the killing fields of the world, I was immersed in stories of forgiveness, redemption, and the resolve to try again. There, I witnessed the juxtaposition of hope in pain, beauty in brokenness, and joy in despair. The paradox of these experiences allowed me to see my debilitating suffering as potential for healing. While I could not control the violence of this world, I realized that the healing of my body was also something that I could not control. And my body had healed to the point where I was strong enough to run again. The more I allowed myself to open up to pain, the more the capacity of my heart expanded. I imagined that if my body could regain its strength, perhaps my heart could too.

Mubanga later told me that she didn't know why she called me before she attempted to take her life at the cemetery. "Perhaps it was God," she said, "who won't let my dreams die." Perhaps God wasn't going to let my dreams die either. Even as I tried to escape them, the dreams of survivors kept calling me back, beckoning me to fight with them, inviting me into the hope I was desperately searching for. I thought that maybe, if Mubanga could try again and live into a new day, I could try again to continue in this work.

The *Lusaka Voice* reported that all medical students failed their exams at the university Mubanga attended. Reporters found that teachers were also unaccredited and unqualified as lecturers, resulting in corruption. In addition, there was an internal system error that miscalculated all of the results for the medical students. The students rioted and blamed the school system for mismanagement.

It seems the work of justice cannot be fulfilled in the absence of suffering.

Perhaps,

God is present in my grief,

present in my anger,

present in my failure,

present in my defeat,

present in my suffering,

present in their suffering.

twelve

BODY WORK

Aᴏғᴛᴇʀ ᴍʏ ᴛʜʀᴇᴇ-ᴍᴏɴᴛʜ-LONG sabbatical concluded, I moved back to the Bay Area just before I turned twenty-five. I felt lucky to be granted another birthday and thought it best to move to a healing space with my family. I spent many mornings with Gung Gung, my grandfather.

"I am happy you're home, it's been long. Lei sik jor faan mei ah?" he asked. I shook my head and removed my shoes at the door. The table was already set with white and blue ceramic bowls and a plate of oranges at the center. He ladled steaming hot jook into our bowls and shuffled to the table. He spoke a blessing over me, thanking God for my safe arrival home. I poured him tea. He sprinkled white pepper, chopped pídàn, and fresh green onions in his bowl and threw a few extra chunks of pídàn into my bowl with his chopsticks. He unfolded the Chinese newspaper and began to read aloud. As he translated the headlines into English for me, his memory of the war returned: stories of near death and survival, the oppression of communism and the brutality of soldiers, the sleepless nights caused by hunger pangs and the sound of explosions. Sharing meals together holds strong significance for togetherness, especially after the mass starvation that Gung Gung grew up in. He recalled how his mother sewed a pocket full of dried fried rice into his jacket, only to be eaten as the final remnant of food should the war separate them.

"The suffering of my boyhood allows me to be grateful in every-thing. Even this jook that I eat every day, I am grateful because it has real meat in it. During the war, my mother gave us salted hot water and jokingly called it 'pork soup' to kindle our imagination and satiate our hungry bellies," he said, chuckling.

"It seems that unfair things in our lives pave the way for good things to come. We must stay strong, persevering as we wait for it. Without faith, there is so much in this world to fear. In fear, there is no joy in living. Joy is what keeps me going. I don't have time to be uptight, life is too short not to laugh," he continued, humming "Blessed Assurance," his favorite hymn.

He always seemed to know what I needed to hear.

After I finished the list of chores he needed me to do around the house, he sent me home with a bag of oranges.

My Chinese American family doesn't show affection through hugging or handholding, as others might. I knew I was loved as a child, but my parents showed it through other ways—like when they would say, "Eat more rice, or you will get sick." "Put a coat on, or you'll freeze." "Get all As, or you won't go to college." These fear-inciting demands were always deeply rooted in love. We were also taught to be careful of our physical surroundings. My father worked as a dentist at a mental hospital. His patients were people who had committed crimes: rape, murder, and other mysterious things. Since childhood, he warned us of the intentions of others; he taught me to always be on guard, because evil does exist in this world—he fixes their teeth.

In my adulthood, I learned to carefully guard my space by choosing not to frequent crowded spaces, to avoid bars full of thirsty eyes and dirty hands, to extend my hand to greet new acquaintances before they could attempt a hug. I watch the ground for shadows following too closely behind mine. I practice muay thai and carry my keys between my knuckles. I thought physical touch was unnecessary, especially since touch too often is unwanted. Always in defense mode, I prepared myself daily to face the external world wearing my armor: black on black and resting bitch face.

Being at home after nearly losing my life was difficult. I felt like I had come back a failure, without stories of triumph or success. When asked how I was doing, I could never admit that I was drowning. Questions like "How are the girls in Africa?" could only be answered politely, to prove that their donations were creating miracles in a relentless cycle of complexities that donors would never know. The truth was that the girls and I were all experiencing pain, but most donors preferred not to hear those stories.

Having to maintain my strong exterior, I was afraid to let anyone know why I had gone on sabbatical. Admitting that my illness was related to my inability to hold such traumatic stories was impossible. I found a therapist, trusting that counseling would allow me the space to express what I was taught to hide. As I confronted my very foreign emotions, the therapist explained that I had taken on the traumatic stories as if they were my own, seen in the nightmares that haunted me and my reactive instincts. I did notice that I was angrier and more irritable, lashing out unjustifiably, pretending depression did not exist in me. Secondary trauma had escalated into physical illness. I was experiencing post-traumatic stress disorder, said my therapist. The process of recognizing this truth was more brutal than the physical illness I had since healed from.

Ten months after my illness, I returned to Kenya for the first time. I found renewed energy after the epiphanies experienced on sabbatical and sessions in therapy, which compelled me to continue my work. I set up back-to-back interviews with girls from

Kakamega to Machakos, all hoping for an opportunity to attend school. Nekesa collected and categorized all of the scholarship applications we received from friends and partnering organizations. We had over thirty qualified applicants, but we only had room for five new scholars. We planned to interview fourteen, and we would choose from there.

Our first interview was with Amani. She came wearing her high school uniform. Her skirt was so sun-bleached and over-washed that it was difficult to tell what color it was before. Her white blouse was perfectly pressed, missing a few buttons, showing her pink top underneath. She wore an oversized sweater that was falling off the shoulders of her small body.

Amani was raped by her teacher when she was thirteen and in her first year of high school. When she realized she was pregnant, she hid for as long as she could, wearing baggy sweaters over her unzipped uniform skirt. One day she passed out while at school, and the school nurse discovered she was seven months pregnant. She was forced to drop out due to the pregnancy. Afraid that she would be blamed for exchanging sex for good grades, she did not tell anyone who the father was. When she gave birth, the teacher that raped her began to threaten her life. Realizing she risked death whether she spoke out or not, she reported the rape with the support of the school nurse. She had been out of school because of the responsibilities of raising her son and having no school fees. Since the attack, she hated wearing her uniform skirt—it was a daily reminder of rape.

Now sixteen, she was determined to return. "I want to become a nurse, to help other girls like that nurse helped me. I want to seek justice for other survivors who haven't been as lucky to go to court," Amani's voice trembled as she spoke.

Amani retained enough evidence through her bloody clothes that her case was opened the same year she was raped. After her son was born, DNA tests confirmed that the perpetrator was the teacher. He was sentenced to twenty-five years in prison.

One after another, the girls came and left. Nekesa and I could only look at each other and sigh, having few words to communicate the heaviness within our hearts. Aspiring lawyers and doctors, social workers and counselors, businesswomen and accountants, they all desired to see a world free of sexual violence. The prospect of receiving academic support gave them the opportunity to dream again, and they left the room with heads held higher than when they came.

By the fourteenth interview, I was emotionally depleted. Their stories of trauma were too much for my small heart to hold. Stepfathers, uncles, pastors—men who crept their way into their houses also crept into their small bodies. They were all children when abused. I couldn't possibly choose which girls should be accepted into our program. I couldn't let them return to the violence that they came from.

I went to bed exhausted and angry, wondering how I could help all of the beautiful faces that I met in the day. While asleep, I felt fingers caressing my skin. I jolted up and gasped, "Who's there?" Staring into the darkness, heart racing, fist clenched, I turned on my bedside lamp and found ants crawling all over my body.

Sleep became an experience of unseen terror. To dodge the terror, I worked late hours with the light on until I fell asleep on the couch. I wasn't afraid of the ants as much as the moving figures who haunted me in my sleep. My father was right: evil does exist, and it found its way into my dreams.

My therapist taught me tapping, or emotional freedom technique, which is the practice of tapping pressure points starting from the top of the head, the third eye center, the temples, cheekbones, upper lip, chin, clavicle, and finally crossing the arms to tap the side body. When the onslaught of anxiety made me feel unsafe, I learned to bring my body back to the present through physical touch. As I practiced this, I became more aware of the scholars' needs for physical touch to bring them back from the memory of traumatic stress.

On the day that Mubanga told me she was drug-raped, I responded with anger and interrogation. My intention was for justice. But that's not what she needed in the moment. No words or actions could remove her pain; she only wanted me to be present in her pain, without attempting to fix it. She just wanted me to give her a hug.

Practicing presence in my own body, I cautiously extended hugs toward the survivors in our community. They all received my hugs warmly, as if it was an embrace they'd been longing for from their mothers, often holding on longer than I did. Perhaps it was a way that I could show them love beyond words, redeeming physical touch with care instead of abuse.

Just as Mubanga held my hand as we maneuvered through Lusaka, I learned to hold her hand as I stumbled through cross-cultural misunderstandings as I learned to advocate better with survivors. Growing in love through physical touch was a way for me to show that I was present with her in her pain, that she was not alone. I began to sense her pain, even when we were apart.

In the morning, I found a text from her.

"Hi Mom. Something happened last night, but I wanted to tell you myself before someone else does."

"Okay, what happened?"

"Rape."

I called her immediately, and she was crying. Her family's house did not have a bathroom within the compound, and so they used the shared bathroom outside of their gate. Before going to bed, she went out to use the bathroom. Just a few feet away from their front gate, two men grabbed her from behind. They wrapped her own chitenge around her head. Hands covered her mouth and stripped her body. This was her third rape.

I did not question, I did not accuse, I did not shame.

But I could not even give her a hug.

After listening to her heavy breaths laden with tears, I told her, "I love you, baby girl. I am holding your pain with you, you are not alone in this, it was not your fault." It was all I could do.

In times like these, I am reminded that I cannot protect her from harm. When I am far away, I can only hold her in love.

*They will try
to blindfold you to erase your divine vision of light,
don't let them.*

*They will try
to grab ahold of your arms—twisting from behind,
    keeping you from reaching out in hope,
don't let them.*

*They will try
to chain shackles of pain to your ankles to debilitate
    your movement toward love,
don't let them.*

*They will try
to silence your voice—the inner voice within, by filling
    your head with strange noises of lies and deceit,
 don't let them.*

*They don't know that
you are stronger,
your voice is louder,
your spirit has power,
and that vision will remain as long as you
let it.*

thirteen

WE ARE GRADUATING

ANGERED, I OVERWORKED myself in Kenya—bouncing from children's homes in the village to family homes in the slum, strategic planning meetings to art workshops with child survivors of sexual abuse. The youngest survivor there was two years old. I plastered a smile on my face as I attended my speaking engagements. I sat in meetings holding my strategic plans together with my anxiety. I covered my neck tension with Tiger Balm. I traveled across the world portraying an image of strength in public while despair weakened my body in private.

As my old patterns started to return, I remembered to breathe life into my lungs. I was rapidly losing weight, so I ate more noodles for long life. I allowed myself to be angry, but I tried not to enact violence as a result of my anger. I resisted the urge to carry lies that I wasn't doing enough. I censored thoughts of inadequacy. I resisted self-blame. I meditated to release my need to control.

I was determined to forge ahead. Though we were only planning to accept five scholars for that year, I accepted ten, including Amani, whose story captured me. This doubled our community to twenty scholars. I couldn't bear rejecting those girls whose faces had been burned into my memory.

I forced myself to search for something good in the everyday. Little things kept me clinging to hope, like the fresh aroma of ripe mangoes. I bought papayas the size of my face and green avocados that were large enough to eat as a meal. I took delight in the smiles of the mamas as we bartered and bantered in Swahili. I spent more time in the tiny homes in Kibera and Mathare, enjoying omena or githeri prepared with love and the friendship of survivors. I played with the neighborhood children to reclaim my sense of innocence. They often invited me into their circle to dance. This time, I couldn't refuse, and I attempted to mimic their movements. We laughed at the gracelessness of my body.

The feeling of failure haunted me still—but this time, I wouldn't allow it to overtake me. I had a graduation to attend.

Mara was finally graduating from university with a degree in journalism. I came with an entourage of scholars from Freely in Hope. Mara's mom proudly wore her best kitenge dress and danced all the way from the bus to the seating area, shouting hallelujahs and chanting in her mother tongue.

"How are you feeling?" I asked Mara's mom, as I put my arm around her.

"Heh! I didn't know. I feel so good. I didn't know that this day would come. We are graduating!" she said with an unbroken smile as she touched her forehead to mine.

Indeed, she deserved a graduation too. After decades of hard labor, the seed of her womb had finally blossomed—her only daughter flourished beyond all expectations.

When Mara came out in full cap and gown, she was unrecognizable, no longer the strung-out seventeen-year-old just trying to survive. That day she was euphoric, and it was better than any high she had experienced before. Mara's mom pulled mshino, tinsel of all colors, out of her purse and draped them around Mara's neck. She also had a picture frame made into a necklace that said, "Congratulations, we are proud of you!" Mara's mom continued in her low-register chanting, marching to the beat of her chant, pumping her shoulders to the rhythm of her voice. As I watched her admire her daughter, I had a flashback to the time that we first met. When Mara could barely utter a word, her mom was present for her. Not knowing the pain of exploitation that brought her to that point of silence, her mother, holding her in unconditional love, became her advocate.

There are many secrets that I hold on behalf of these daughters. I've been told stories that their own mothers do not know, could not know, for it would break them. With insufficient hands, I try to hold these stories on behalf of their mothers. Instead, I break for them.

I believe that mothers always do the best that they can with what they have. Even as they try to protect their daughters and balance freedom with autonomy, there is still so much that is out of their control. Uncles, fathers, pastors, and teachers creep their way in, offering twenty cents, a cup of unga, a packet of milk. When vital resources are allotted to some and not others, the field of mothering becomes unfair.

Mothers—
they risk and work,
they hold back and release,
they praise and shame,
they incite fear and model courage,
they hide tears and laugh freely,
they break down and build walls,
they create barriers around the gardens they plant,
they love in the ways they know how.

Yet even within the confines of well-intended protection, the violence of the world seems to find its way through these woman-made walls.

Mara's mom did the best she knew how. Because of this, Mara, in return, would do anything for her mother, even risk her own body to ensure that her mother's body was strong.

Love looks like food on the table. Neither Mara nor her mom will ever know what the other did to get the food there.

Though Mara's graduation seemed like the paramount event in her story, I reveled in the little victories that got us here, like when she accidentally shared her story with me over chai, when she decided to drink soda as a replacement for cocaine, when she chose to register for night classes to avoid hustling on the streets, when I saw her laugh uninhibited for the first time. I watched these scenes unfold in real time, witnessing the glorious process that brought us thus far.

Mara draped her graduation gown over Amani and told her, "One day, it'll be your turn, and we'll be dancing for you." Amani looked up at her in awe. Mara cried as she laughed and pointed her finger at me, "If you told me when we met that I would one day graduate from university, I would have blown smoke into your face and have told you to wake up—you're dreaming."

She held her graduation cap to the sky and looked at it in disbelief. "When we first met, I was so high. Even at that time, you believed in me when I didn't believe in myself. My transformation happened because you didn't give up on me. I promise you, this will not be the last graduation that you attend."

I took a boda boda taxi home and allowed the cool air to sweep through my hair. We sped in between cars stuck in traffic. My hands gripped tightly to the back of the seat. While being jostled around, I leaned back to look up at the vast sky and watched the cloud formations move effortlessly above. New patterns were beginning to form, transforming fear of failure and allowing hope to rise again. Transformation will come, Mara reminded me, don't give up.

We are graduating.

I have been there before—in battle,
in tension, in war.

I know far too well that this work of
justice requires sacrifice—in blood,
in sweat, in tears.

My wounds are still exposed.

And when I see my children follow
closely behind, I am proud.

But at the same time, I desperately
want to tell them, "Come, but don't."

For their skin tone, their accent, their
gender places a target on their backs.

And at the same time,

I know far too well that their backs
were built to uphold—to uphold
justice for the multitudes of children
who look just like them.

Before I can turn around to speak,

I see them running beside me and
pushing back the darkness before me.

fourteen

TUKO PAMOJA?

NEKESA'S DAUGHTER, HOPE, was turning nine. I threw her a birthday party and invited all the scholars to come. I folded paper into cones to make party hats. I made a string of banners to hang in all the windows. I bought a bunch of oranges and displayed them in bowls made of acacia wood. I made Nekesa's favorite Chinese dishes: steamed tilapia and a chopped cucumber salad garnished with raw garlic and peanuts.

Hope sat in the center of the room, drawing with broken crayons and enjoying the attention from all the beautiful women around her. Amani was there, sitting quietly and drawing flowers with Hope. We danced, we ate, we celebrated the gifts that Hope gave us all.

Nekesa took an orange and began to peel it. "Nekesa!" I yelled, "those are my decorations!"

Nekesa's eyes widened. The girls laughed hysterically, not understanding why I would put oranges on the table if they were not meant to be eaten.

"It's for good luck and prosperity for the birthday girl!" I explained. Then I said, "I'm just kidding, you can eat it." Everyone took an orange.

"How's your house coming along in the village?" I asked Nekesa.

"It took a long time, but brick by brick, the walls are finally finished. I just sent money home for the roof!" Her eyes shifted and I could tell she wanted to change the subject.

Amani stood up and interrupted us, "Everyone, everyone. I have something to say. Ladies, please quiet down. Tuko pamoja? Are we together?" I was surprised that Amani would call attention to herself in front of us. We waited with anticipation. "I am going to perform an improvisation piece. It's called 'Decoration.' Sit back, relax, and enjoy." She said as she bowed.

You see, here there is a bowl of beautiful oranges.
There are people who think that those oranges are for eating,
I'm sorry to tell you, but those are not for eating.
My friends, they are for decoration!

The room roared in laughter. We laughed until we cried.

Amani's voice no longer trembled when she spoke. Just one year ago, when Amani came to her scholarship interview, she could barely say her name without it being followed by tears of shame. But today she lit up our hearts with pride. Amani surprised us all with the gift of laughter.

I looked around the room at each girl's face. When they laughed, they became little girls again, reclaiming their innocence. I savor moments like these, amazed at how much they've grown in confidence, in sass, in humor, in freedom, in love for each other. I held my hand over my laughing belly in gratitude.

It had been six years since Freely in Hope began, and it had become more than I ever imagined it would be. The growing leadership of our scholars was astounding. Healing was taking place, and the transformation was evident. Our community outreach programs were led by survivors, with Nekesa and Mara leading the way in Kenya. Their sense of empowerment contributed to the greater vision. They imagined new programs that equipped women in prostitution with options for alternative work, curricula that taught high school students about consent, and workshops that taught children that they have autonomy over their bodies. The scholars made up a song that says, "These are my private parts, private parts, private parts. These are my private parts, no one can touch!" In teaching children this song, we dispel the myth that their bodies are not their own. We also teach them to tell someone they trust if their boundaries are violated. Our scholars were adamant about doing more outreach with children, since the majority of them were raped before they turned fourteen.

Freely in Hope began from a single story. Not knowing where the story would lead, survivors and advocates banded together to create this organization. Six years later, our little organization had grown to serve twenty girls in the scholarship program. Through their leadership, we were able to reach over two thousand people across Kenya that year. We imagined how much further we could go together, pamoja.

But though Nekesa laughed in public, she was grieving in silence. Hope's ninth birthday also marked ten years since Nekesa was raped. The anniversary of the trauma led her back to a familiar place.

Over the school holiday, Nekesa sent Hope to Ebutayi to spend time with her grandmother. Since Nekesa graduated from university, she began to earn her father's respect—mostly because she was sending money home to build a house for her mom. Her father took most of it to spend on busaa. Nevertheless, Nekesa's generosity was an attempt to reconcile with her family, which allowed Hope to know her roots. But when Hope came back home from Ebutayi, something was different. She was no longer buoyant with curiosity. Having gone through our training for children, Hope said that her cousin touched her private parts. Nekesa was furious and switched back to survival mode. Grieved that she was unable to protect her daughter from the same violence she experienced, she sought to protect herself from others whom she thought might bring harm. I was one of them.

I was traveling in the United States when I got a phone call from Nekesa, yelling, "You are raising all this money, and I am not seeing any of it! You have never cared for me, and you are using my story to make money for yourself! I will not tolerate this exploitation any longer! I quit!" She hung up.

Six years of blood, sweat, and tears on her behalf could not overcome this festering lie. There were verbal threats and text threats, hate mail and public statements, all accusing me of mismanagement of funds. She questioned my values, my faith, my career, my so-called advocacy for survivors. She threatened to take me to court.

I was devastated that she would accuse me of taking from the very thing I had devoted my life to. She would never know that I didn't receive a salary for the first five years so that all could be invested into what we were building together, or that I couldn't afford health insurance because I put the money toward her graduation, or that I limited what I ate so I could spend that money on food for Hope's party. She would never know how much I believed in her.

I asked myself, *where had I gone wrong?* How could six years of building trust lead to this? Again, I felt that I failed in my leadership.

I came to learn that ever since I was away on sabbatical, she had been taking the organization's money. Every month, when I sent funds for the scholars' academic needs, Nekesa reserved some for herself. With the remains, she limited the benefits that the scholars should have received. This was what she was using to build her mom's house in the village. I felt betrayed that after so many years of journeying together, it came to this.

But I also understood. For those who have received abuse, sometimes it feels safer to anticipate abuse. Leaving was an attempt to shield herself from potential harm, a way of regaining her autonomy, an act of removing herself from the traumatic triggers of the work. If I wanted anything for her, it was for her to achieve greater things than I ever could. And she did.

When we first met, I never would have dreamed that we would make it this far—celebrating the many graduations, the countless survivors who came forward as a result of her courage, the beautiful insights that have strengthened my understanding of what survivor-leadership looks like. She taught me many things about the world that I didn't know I needed to learn. She taught me even at the risk of betrayal to love anyway.

Before then, I had never been accused of a crime that I did not commit.

I know,

*I can do better to speak only words
that give life.*

*I can do better to think thoughts that
always affirm and uplift. I can do better
to listen carefully to the tone of your
voice—trying to understand stories that
are not mine, seeing the fears you've
tried to hide, sensing the spirit of your
presence, catching hidden lessons of
hope unfolding from within.*

I know,

*I have not been able to catch it all—
for its redemptive beauty is far beyond
that which I can comprehend.*

Just know,

*that I will be better at listening,
at understanding, at learning, at
speaking truth, at extending my arms—*

*ready to catch whatever you choose
to share and*

ready to catch you

should you need me there.

fifteen

INVISIBLE WOUNDS

I HAD FULL-BLOWN TANTRUMS up until I was eight years old, in supermarkets, at church, at home. I cried angry tears until I would hyperventilate. It was not a good look. Still, I persisted in the kicking and screaming to prove I was right.

One time, I fell asleep in the car, and my mom left me there because I was too big for her to carry into the house. When I woke up, I was so angry that my mom didn't take me out of the car. I screamed for her to come for me, but she didn't. I dragged my body into the living room, allowing my voice to echo throughout the house. After a few moments, there was still no response. So I threw my body onto the tile floors and flailed my limbs. In my mind, I was trying to flail so hard that I would eventually lift my physical body out of the anger that I felt in my heart.

Finally, I saw my mother with a video camera in hand. While I was still screaming, she played the video back for me and made me watch myself.

I stopped mid-scream, realizing how out of control I was in my body. I never had a temper tantrum again. In that way, at least.

In my childhood, shouting angrily at my sister or jumping off couches in joy would be met with a stern "That's not ladylike" from my mother. I felt like I couldn't be the full expression of myself—laughter, joy, anger, and all. Because I was always reprimanded for my outbursts of anger, I tried to suppress it, thinking that anger was a deadly sin. But suppressing it only meant that it bubbled up later, causing godless words to emerge from my enraged belly. My screaming was now replaced with words that cut through the heart.

After being raped for the third time, Mubanga cut her wrists to feel anything other than that something was inherently wrong with her. When night terrors dragged her back to the past, cutting brought her back to the present. It was an effort to regain control over what was stolen from her. Cutting disrupted the paralyzing flashbacks and allowed her to feel again; seeing blood reminded her that she was still alive.

I often received pictures of her bloody wrists, sent with apologies.

One night, I was in a backstage bathroom, preparing to speak to a room full of a thousand youth leaders, when my phone buzzed. It was a text of another bloody image from Mubanga. I called her back immediately with only few minutes left before going on stage. She didn't answer. She texted me back, "I don't want to talk." I texted back, "Call me back, now." She called back because she knew I was upset. I wanted to reel off my concern for her health, to reaffirm her future vision for herself, to express my love through encouragement, and to show how I desperately wanted her to protect herself from harm. While this was my intent, the words that flew out of my mouth were, "What the hell is wrong with you? Why are you doing this to yourself? Are you an idiot?"

Heat rose to the top of my head as shame washed over me. Somehow, my intention to love came out in violent words. I wasn't angry at her; I was angry at the injustice of it all—that the violence of the world caused her to enact violence on herself.

"I feel like you just poured cold water on my head. I'm already drowning, Mom," she responded, her voice numb.

I've never physically harmed myself, only in my mind. I've recited untruths as if they were labels across my forehead. I've condemned myself for what I could not control. While I didn't take out my anger by cutting wounds across my flesh, my anger manifested itself in words that I regretted. And they too created scarring. Though I tried with all my might, I would say words I didn't mean and fail to say the ones that I did.

I apologized as quickly as she would hear it. "What do you want me to do?" I asked helplessly.

"Mom, just love me. You've taught me everything I need to know. I have to fight this one on my own."

My fist was clenched. She was right.

I rolled the sleeves up on my white blazer and stepped on stage.

My mom and I drove to Sacramento to visit my aunt. I told her how upset I had been with the systems of injustice that we are forced to work under. We encountered obstacle after obstacle, and it seemed as if we kept losing.

I had just heard that Amani's case was recently appealed. After the perpetrator spent five years in prison, he paid big money for a lawyer to fight for his innocence. The basis of the appeal was proving that Amani was not a minor when they had sex; therefore it was consensual. They brought a fake birth certificate to court that dated Amani much older than she was. Court date after court date, Amani showed up ready to testify, but the hearings were pushed back because the perpetrator was sick. They released him from prison due to his illness, but he was not sick. They even saw each other on the same matatu. He looked at her with a smirk, and Amani stared him down, blood boiling, waiting for her justice to come again. When the new court date came, the lawyer tried every trick he could to manipulate Amani. But she wouldn't blink. As big as he was, he was no match for her. Though her voice was quiet, her words were loud, amplified by countless other girls who have not had opportunities to speak their truth in court. She carried their courageous voices with her, and he was outnumbered.

"He was already convicted, already in prison, already serving time when dirty money was able to get him out on bail. Now he is running around Nairobi while Amani is hiding in fear that he will kill her so that his case will be cleared." My voice escalated as I iterated the story to my mom. I realized I was speeding, so I slowed down. "The world is unfair to those who have already endured enough pain."

My mom was silent. After a few breaths, she turned to me and said, "I now know why you were so angry as a child. You knew that all was not well with the world, but you didn't know how to respond. And so you would react in tantrums and yelling, fighting and screaming. But somehow, you've been able to channel your anger toward something meaningful—toward justice."

My mother's words felt like redemption. All of my life, I was taught that the anger that I carried needed to be suppressed. But perhaps anger is not a deadly sin, nor is it the enemy of love. Rather, it is the heart of love showing deep desire for justice through a visceral reaction in the body.

And if anger is doing the work of love, then I must allow myself to feel.

To feel anger that causes my bones to shake and voice to raise,

To feel anger that prepares my heart and mind for a long fight,

To feel anger toward unjust systems that cater to the privileged,

To feel anger at the sexism of our world that sees women only as objects of exploitation,

To feel anger that women are not safe, even in our own bodies,

To feel anger that does not inflict violence on self or others, but

To feel anger that will allow myself to feel something else: the expansion of my heart.

*I would never choose to harm you,
like others have. For I try to listen and
understand, practicing patience and
generosity, a little more today than
yesterday. Try as I might, I fail time and
time again. The familiarity of anger and
shame are constantly there—biting the
back of my throat, attempting to escape.
While good intention sits at the pit of
my belly, it surfaces much later, when
it's too late, when those ungodly words
have already escaped and ghostly
memories return to the present.
They haunt me in my sleep.*

*For as my heart's capacity for love
might expand, there are remnants
of my heart still unformed—its broken
pieces are unable to fill the space it
occupies. When anger and fear manifest
themselves in words that reduce to ash,
I forget. I forget that women—mothers
—are made of fire, holding the potential
to both burn and balm, harm and
heal, enclose and illuminate,
conceal and clarify, exhaust
and embrace. It is this same fire that
can mold fear into double-edged
weapons with intentions to protect.*

*Always, with intentions to protect
against the violence of darkness.*

*This darkness will choose to
harm you, like others have—
attempting to destroy your light.*

But try as it might, it will fail.

*For your light was birthed from this
same place where women—daughters
—are made of fire.*

*Daughter, your fire holds the potential
to either burn or balm the cracks
between your broken heart, to harm
or heal the darkened skin across
your arms, to enclose or illuminate
hopeful visions of your future self,
to exhaust or embrace the woman
you are becoming.*

*Fists clenched for the cross punch,
simultaneously holding close and
letting go—*

*I release you into dreams much
greater than my own.*

sixteen

CALL ME BY MY NAME

AFTER HEARING ABOUT Amani's appealed case, I returned to Kenya. I was also scheduled to speak with a group of women working in prostitution in Kisumu, Western Kenya. I asked Mara to join me because of her desire to do more outreach work with women who came from the same background as her.

Mara and I found each other where matatu numbers 46 and 32 meet in Nairobi's bustling central business district. "Stay close and watch your bag," she said to me as we maneuvered through alleyways lined with street hawkers. I held my breath every time we passed between the bumpers of massive buses, their engines rumbling. Finding our matatu, the conductors yelled out some numbers and pushed us into our seats.

Settling in, I pulled out House of Manji biscuits. "Do you want some? I'm starving, I haven't eaten today," I said as I started to munch. It wasn't even 10 a.m.

"No, I haven't eaten either. I think it's rude to eat on the matatu. That is the worst feeling—when you're starving and people on the matatu are eating french fries that you can't afford." I swallowed the gritty pieces left in my mouth and put it away.

As we jerked our way out of town, we passed through an affluent neighborhood along Waiyaki Way. "I had a client who lived in that fancy apartment," she recalled. "One time I desperately needed to find medicine for my mom. I told him about it, and he gave me some money—without questions or expectations. It wasn't a loan because he still paid me for my services the next time I saw him."

I wondered how many times I chose not to extend generosity to my friends who were forced to find other means of survival.

The next morning, we arrived at the church in Kisumu to find the women's organization that hosted us. There were around forty women, all who looked like they were well over forty-five years old, though some of them had not yet reached thirty. These women had been working on the streets for at least a decade, bearing multiple children as a result, struggling to feed the mouths of their babies in addition to themselves, attempting to combat HIV with antiretroviral drugs. Some of them were raising their daughters to work in the only way they knew how. In sharing Freely in Hope's mission with them, we hoped that they could imagine their daughters breaking the cycle of generational prostitution.

As the heat from the sun beat down on the tin roof above, the air was heavy with the weight of their pain. Mara and I stood in front of these grown women feeling incredibly inexperienced. They stared back at us unimpressed. We wondered what advice could possibly soften their defenses.

Mara shared her story of the new possibilities she experienced after six years of working in prostitution. She started by handing out pieces of paper with the words *slut, hoe, prostitute, eshitwatsi, good for nothing, unworthy, unlovable*. As each person read what was on their paper, Mara said, "I don't know if anyone else can identify with these words, but these were all labels that were placed on me." She recounted the rapes that led her to work in prostitution not by choice but by desperation. Not for herself but for her mother's health and her nieces' school fees. Not for extravagance but for an education. Not for love but for hope of something better. As she confidently projected her voice, she looked at me often, as if waiting for nonverbal approval. I nodded and *mmmed* as often as I could to let her know I was present, even though I didn't understand all of her Swahili. She pleaded with the mothers in the room, "Please do not let your daughters suffer from the same pain as you."

After Mara so powerfully shared her story, the women began to ask her questions: Are you HIV positive? How old were you when you started prostituting? What kind of drugs were you on? Does your mom know you were a prostitute? What does she think about it? Did she do anything to help you?

As the questions started to escalate, I could see that Mara was feeling uncomfortable by the storm of interrogation, especially as it related to her mom. Mara looked at me, this time signaling for help. Suddenly, the rain began pouring down, pounding against the tin roof. She exhaled with relief. Mara was saved by the rain, and we broke for lunch.

The women served us Royco-flavored stew over rice. Mara and I sat together in silence, listening to the pouring rain, wondering what to do next. We had no appetite. "My mother can never know my story. It will kill her," she whispered. Triggered by the barrage of questioning, Mara was exhausted and didn't want to speak again. She felt rejected by the very women she had attempted to offer relief to. The women were guarded, and I was afraid that our presence would come with expectations for sponsorship for their children. I knew that we could not afford school fees for all of their children—and if we couldn't offer hope in that way, by what other means could we?

Moments later, the rain stopped and the heat of the sun beat down on us once again. The women waited for Mara to answer their questions, but I stood up instead to ask, "How do you all feel?"

A woman raised her hand. "Pained. I am imagining that Mara is my daughter, and I do not want my daughter to go through the same pain." The women hummed in agreement.

"Remember the labels that were written on these papers?" I asked as I held up the derogatory names that Mara started with. "Mara no longer identifies with these names because she found her purpose. Part of that purpose was going back to school so that she could reach her dream—a dream that has always been outside of prostitution. The other part of that purpose is sharing her story with you. Our hope today is that you might find the courage to dream again, for yourselves and for your daughters."

I invited the women to close their eyes, and we took a few deep breaths together. I thought I'd share the same breath prayer that released me from the labels I gave myself. "Imagine that God is calling you by name. What is God's name for you?"

Out of silence came tears. I heard their voices confidently say, "I hear that I am a business woman." "I am a hairdresser." "I am loved." "I am strong." "I am valuable." "I am a good mother."

We rested in our collective understanding that we are more than the labels that have been placed on us. After our meeting was over, the woman who raised her hand first came up to us. "I have a daughter who used to work with me. I don't want her to continue in this same pain because I am HIV positive. I'd like you to meet—it's not too late for her. Her name is Akinyi."

The next day we held interviews with girls who applied for our scholarship program in this region. Akinyi came into her interview with tremendous poise and confidence. Her Afro was combed into a perfect halo. "My mom told me about your story," she said to Mara. "I have a story similar to tell." I was shocked to learn that she was seventeen, for she carried herself with a maturity that could only come from her experiences.

As the eldest, Akinyi grew up taking care of her two younger sisters while her mother went out looking for work. Akinyi would often fetch water for the neighbors, hoping that they would share some of their food as payment. As a child, Akinyi didn't know what type of work her mother did except that she was out of the house both day and night. One night while her mom was working, two men came to the house looking for her mother. When they didn't find her, they raped Akinyi instead. She was twelve.

When Akinyi was sixteen, her mom was diagnosed with cancer. The pastor from their church came to their house every night to pray for her mom's healing. One day, he told them that they needed to fast and pray for one week in order to receive complete healing. The fast would take place at his house in the Kakamega Forest. Since her mother was bedridden, Akinyi went on her mother's behalf. She was picked up by a boda boda and taken to a thatch-roof house. She found the pastor and his family eating. After dinner, the wife and children went to sleep. Akinyi asked, "I thought we were supposed to be fasting for my mom's healing." The pastor said, "The fast will begin tomorrow; we will start praying now." Akinyi bowed her head, and the pastor said that God had revealed to him in a vision that Akinyi's family was tied with evil spirits of sickness and prostitution. "The only way to receive healing for this, as instructed by God, is to sleep with me." Akinyi opened her eyes in disbelief.

"He turned into a monster," she said, wrestling her to the floor and raping her. Akinyi fought back, calling for help, but no one came. When he was done, he gave her a white cloth and dirty hair. "Burn these," he said, "then the evil spirits will flee." He left her alone to pray as she burned away the evil that had penetrated her body. At dawn, he found Akinyi crying, pleading to go home. He said, "Only if you do not tell anyone." She agreed, and he brought her home. To hide the secret, she pretended that the fasting was hard for her, which is why her body was weak and her spirit was low.

After that, she continued to suffer at the hands of multiple abusers—her teacher, the school principal's husband, a sponsor who paid for her school fees. Yet she finished high school with above-average marks. To support her sisters' education, she followed in her mother's footsteps. While her mother's money went to alcohol, Akinyi paid for her sisters' tuition fees. She would rather pimp out her own body in order to protect her sisters.

After high school, she learned how to plait hair and worked at a local hair salon, which became the skill that saved her. She found courage to file a report against the pastor who raped her after hearing stories of other women who had similarly been assaulted by him. Akinyi's dream was to be a lawyer. "Being a survivor, I would like to help others through the journey of healing and to be a part of bringing justice to the girl child."

I knew she would be a perfect fit for our growing community of survivor-leaders.

After meeting Akinyi, Mara was ecstatic, realizing that the power of her story was creating freedom for survivors like her. That night, Mara reflected on the importance of storytelling: "Stories of violence are so hard to tell. Every time we talk about the things that hurt us, it feels like we are experiencing the trauma again, but the truth is, healing comes by telling and retelling the things that hurt us most. Too often, survivors don't have the courage to believe in their own story. They fear that they will be judged. I've been a victim of this until I realized that every time I share, I am taking another step toward healing. If my story can impact just one person, then all my experiences of heartache and pain were worth it. If I have to go through hell to bring Akinyi out of it, I will."

I would have never imagined that I would witness such incredible transformation in Mara. The little girl who would not talk now used her voice to liberate others, giving them a new name.

"The women we met today inspired me so much. I've been thinking about it, and I want people to call me by my birth name, Mara-Anne. Mara was my street name, and it reminds me of all the labels people placed on me. But Mara-Anne is the name my mother gave to me, and I want to honor it as a symbol of who I am becoming."

Mara-Anne had such a groundbreaking experience that she said, "We should do this internationally! I want my story to help more girls who are stuck in prostitution. I already have my passport!" I was surprised to hear this, because passports don't come easily for people living in the slums. I also recalled an email she sent me years ago, lamenting the fact that she needed a passport to apply for a job with an airline company. She said she got it when she was working in the brothel. Her pimp told her that instead of making one dollar in Kenya per night, she would make one hundred dollars in America per night. With the promise of work in America, her pimp got her a passport and was waiting to get the visa for America.

When the opportunity for university came up with Freely in Hope, she left the brothel for good. Had she gotten her visa, she would have left for the United States, leaving her future education behind. I was stunned and said, "Do you know that you were almost trafficked to America?"

She asked, "What's that?"

I explained to her that human trafficking is the movement of people from one place to another, where they are exploited for sex or labor for little to no pay. The cost of transportation is so high that the trafficked person is rarely able to pay off the debt that accumulates. "You're essentially prostituting for free."

"Ghai!" she exclaimed in disbelief.

We sat in silence, both of us feeling so incredibly grateful to be free.

When the shadows of my former self
follow me into the light,

It will finally see
that life in all its beauty
was there all along.

It was mine to claim.

seventeen

ON RETREAT

COMING BACK TO NAIROBI, I prepared for our annual retreat where we would bring together all of our scholars from the various schools they studied at. At our three-day retreats, we learn, share stories of hope, and grow together.

I flew Mubanga and Ruby from Zambia to Kenya for the first time. Since Mubanga's most recent rape, I wanted her to be in community with the rest of our Kenyan girls as a reminder that she was not alone.

I found Ruby pushing Amani higher and higher on the swing, yelling, "Fly with your wings, Amani! Fly!" The girls love pushing each other on the swings, feeling a rise within their bodies. They become children again, like they were before abuse forced them to grow up too quickly.

As I had always envisioned that Freely in Hope would be led by survivors, I trained them in leadership throughout the years. This would be the first time that the scholars would lead at the retreat. Mara-Anne led a storytelling workshop, Akinyi led a workshop on legal rights, and Mubanga led a dance class. Ruby was to preach on Sunday morning, and Amani was to share her testimony for the first time.

◆ ❈ ◆

A quiet knock on my door woke me up from my sleep. It was Mubanga. "I had a flashback, and I'm scared." She crawled into bed with me and shut her eyes tightly, whimpering. Her body trembled. "I keep seeing shadows that are trying to rape me." I held her and reminded her, "You're in a safe place, you're in a safe place . . ." She attempted to rock herself back to sleep, but moments later, she was startled by another flashback. She jumped out of bed and went back to her room.

Half asleep, I rolled out of bed to make sure she was okay. I had become extravigilant because of her frequent cutting. The light was on, and she sat staring into nothing. "Are you okay?" I asked.

She jumped, startled at the sound of my voice. "Yes, I'm just going to write lyrics to a song I'm working on now. I'm afraid to turn the light off." She reached for my hand to assure me that she was going to be okay. "Look," she said, pointing to the lines of fresh scars on her wrist, "they're healing already."

Ruby was sleeping in the same room. She woke up and asked, "Mom, can you get me something to put dirt in tomorrow? I need it for my sermon."

"Yes. Go back to sleep." I kissed them both and left them with the light on.

Sunday morning at breakfast I made sure the lid to the strawberry jam was closed before Mara came down. I saved a piece of mandazi for Mubanga because I knew she was going to be late. I found a kitchen tray to hold the dirt for Ruby.

The scholars led our Sunday service. They all gathered in a circle, wearing their best kitenge dresses, and started to sing and clap, to dance and shout. Mubanga and Ruby tied kitenge around their waists and danced in the center. Others waved their kitenge like banners to spur them on. My greatest joy is to see them like this: free and uninhibited, swaying and stomping with eyes

closed and hearts open, spirits colliding in unified pain and in-
fectious joy.

Amani stood and walked to the center to share her testimony.
She was wearing a kitenge skirt and colorful Maasai-beaded
sandals. I had complimented her on her sandals that morning.
She immediately took them off her feet and attempted to give
them to me. I refused. She insisted, "Remember when you used
to wear those cloth shoes with holes in them?" She said with a
gentle smile, "I wasn't sure how our school fees would be paid,
but look at how far we've come!"

Amani's long braids were hidden in a head wrap that made her
look like a woman with confidence greater than Erykah Badu's.

"This morning, I woke up with the courage to wear a skirt."
The girls snapped their fingers. This was the first time Amani
wore a skirt on her own volition since she was raped by her
teacher. The stigma of "What were you wearing?" or "Why
couldn't you run?" had oppressed her long enough. After testi-
fying in court a dozen times, she had become certain of her truths.
Wearing a skirt was an act of reclaiming power over her body. It
was a symbol of defiance.

"I will no longer live in fear because of him," she stated confidently. "Even though I won my case five years ago and the rapist
is out on probation, I will still use my voice to speak my truth. I
will not back down!" Her statement was met with exuberant
clapping and ululations from the rest of us. Amani looked at each
one of us as if daring us to reclaim our own bodies as well. I
looked up at her in awe.

Next Ruby delivered her sermon with fire. "God handpicked
you. You have a special power that differentiates you from everybody
else. That power is our stories. When we tell our stories, we are
liberated. We no longer identify with the labels that the world
places on us. People in my community labeled me as a prostitute,
a dirty girl who would be good for nothing but prostitution.

But God has given me mercy. Yes, I was working in prostitution so that I can pay for my school fees, but no, I am not a prostitute. I am here now, studying in university and receiving God's mercy. That's what I should be talking about.

"It's so profound—that God loves me so much, that he accepts me, that he places value on me, that he surrounds me with a community like this one! Surrounded by the love of God and this community, I overcame the pain of being raped. I overcame the pain of humiliation. I overcame the pain of self-doubt. This pain that I have now? I can overcome it. When you fall, stand up, dust yourself off, and choose to move forward. Because you are capable of far better things than the world has condemned us to."

Her voice deepened with passion that shook me. Ruby asked the girls to write the labels that people had given them in the past. Each girl wrote them down on a piece of paper, burned it, and placed it in the tray of dirt.

"God is always with us, in us, right here in our hearts. It's for us to recognize that God is always present, always near, always loving. Even in our brokenness, we must stand up and live into our rewritten stories."

She asked Mubanga to sing:

Pass me not, O gentle Savior,
Hear my humble cry;
While on others Thou art calling,
Do not pass me by.

We squatted together in a circle, watching our labels of oppression go up in flames. Ruby's story was opening up new revelation and opportunities for healing—specifically for Mubanga in her sleepless nights and moments of immense terror. Just three years earlier, Mubanga and Ruby had met. Then, it was Mubanga's story that brought healing for Ruby. Today, the healing words were returned.

Watching the interchange between Ruby and Mubanga, I closed my eyes to bask in the feeling of redemption, and I felt someone wipe my wet cheeks with their hands.

After the service, Akinyi came to me and buried her face in my chest, sobbing. "I wanted to tell you before, but I was so ashamed. After I tried to file a rape case against the pastor, I found out that there was nothing they could do. It was so hard retelling that story to the police—what was the point of me even trying? They ridiculed me for something that I didn't do. How can I be an advocate against sexual violence for others when I can't even be an advocate for myself?"

As I felt her grief wash over me, I let my questions overflow into tears of disbelief and anger, then compassion and care. I held her cheeks in my hands. "You're still the same strong girl that I know," I told her, and I felt the weight of her head drop into my palms.

We piled the girls into a rickety matatu to drop them off in town. As we drove off, I remembered that we had left the cake in the fridge. It's the cake to celebrate all of the birthdays for that school term. For most of them, this is the only cake they receive for their birthdays. We quickly turned around to get the cake. In the car, I cut up pieces of the homemade cake as the girls sang, "Cut the cake, sia ugali (it's not ugali), cut the cake, sia ugali . . ." I passed out the pieces, and the birthday girls gave birthday speeches.

I left them to their excited chatter in Swahili and pulled out the checkbook. We were running late on depositing checks for the scholars' tuition fees because we didn't have enough money in the bank. I was afraid that if we didn't pay on time, they would be sent home. This has happened to them too many times in their lives, and I could not let that happen to them with us. Mara-Anne was going to help me deposit them in town that day.

I felt a tap on my shoulder. "Mom, here," Amani said as she fed me a piece of cake with her hands.

Mara-Anne helped me list off the checks to write for the scholars. Just as I finished, I looked up and saw that we were almost in town, and I said, "Phew, we made it right on time!" Mara-Anne and I laughed at ourselves—how we were singing happy birthday at the top of our lungs, passing out pieces of cake, and writing checks for the schools in a rickety matatu. As we pulled up to the bus station, the girls piled out, full of energy. They lined up to hug me goodbye. We were all sad to leave each other but happy to have been together. As Mara-Anne left with checks in hand, she turned around to say, "God must smile upon you as you sleep."

I could only hope that she was right.

How lucky are we—

that we experience miracles
on the daily.

Like how these mountains
that seemed so far away,
we conquered today.

Like how this vast ocean,
so largely treacherous,
we crossed together.

Like how these dangerous winds
carried us to the place that

we are in today.

eighteen

BEAUTY IN BROKENNESS

Mubanga leaned against my knees as I helped her undo her braids. Her sister Grace used to plait her hair under the mango tree at home. As children, Mubanga and her sisters would climb mango trees as if the limbs were their own. Mango trees were abundant—every home had at least one mango tree for shade in the hot season and fruit in the harvest season. She laughed as she remembered other moments of her childhood and recalled the games she played as a child using nothing but rhythm and the movement of their bodies. I watched the scar lines on her wrist flick back and forth as she pulled out her braids. I knew we had to talk about her cutting, but I waited for her to bring it up.

"When I was little, my sister and I would make dolls out of dirt to play with. We would pour water onto the dirt and mix it to the right consistency to create clay. After molding our little girls and boys, we would leave them in the sun to dry before we could play with them. We had to be patient in the drying process, otherwise the dolls would break. But if it broke, I would simply add more water to join it together again, and I would have to wait patiently some more. And you know how impatient I can be!" We laughed, knowing it was true for both of us.

"I am like the little girl made out of mud. I am in process," she continued. "In this process, some of life's hard lessons are going to stick and some are not. But it doesn't mean that I'm not going to be the woman I'm supposed to be. I am fragile, and parts of me might break, but that doesn't mean that I cannot be made whole again. Sometimes, I'll need to wait for the process of drying so that I am strong to walk again, to be made beautiful and whole. Mom?"

"Yes, I'm here," I responded.

"Don't give up on me. Even beautiful things can break if they're overused and mistreated. I break a lot, but I am strong. I know my purpose. That is what keeps me going. This hope is the water, the bond that keeps rejoining the broken but beautiful pieces of me."

She revealed that she had big news for me. Since her medical program was cited for mismanagement, I wanted her to move schools, and she wanted to change her field of study. Initially she wanted to be a doctor to bring her family honor and prestige. But this was not her desire. Instead of seeing one person at a time, she wanted to do something that brought lasting change to communities under the weight of systemic injustice.

"I have put some of the broken pieces of my dreams back together to create my future. I want to study public policy. I think I will have a greater impact if I study how policies can change our broken systems. These systems that I have grown up under have silenced girls long enough. Leaders cannot understand the harmful dynamics that surround girls in rural areas if they've never been through it! They keep producing solutions that aren't even in our favor, and it angers me! I believe that it's time that we speak out against them. I want to be part of the mending process. The little girls in my community deserve better than what I went through," she said with firm belief.

I pulled out the last braid and fluffed her hair to even it out. She took a deep breath in to allow her scalp to breathe. Her hand reached for mine. She lifted her head to the skies and smiled, "It will soon be harvest season at home, I can almost smell it."

Something in my chest felt like it was expanding with light the color of mangoes. I squeezed her hand to let her know that I could almost smell it too.

◆ ✳ ◆

Sacred moments like these mend me back together. In the courage of their voices, the hope of their careers, their vision for the world, the strength of their will, their anger mending injustice, the power of their being—these are the moments where love abides.

Daily, my work requires me to delve into the hellish reality of unimaginable experiences of abuse. Neither words nor images can fully convey the emotional crises, psychological torment, and heart-wrenching pain that my daughters in these places have been forced to endure. When I feel like giving up under the weight of violent injustice, I am reminded of their dreams. They graciously extend themselves on behalf of others through their advocacy efforts, their academic and career pursuits, and their compassion for other little girls who are versions of themselves. Their shared experiences with me give me hope to live into the new day, pursuing the call toward justice once more.

I have learned from their voices that speak truth into dark places. The voices arising from places of oppression provide hope for healing, for liberation, for me. These are the stories that have transcended my being; they have unlocked my angry heart that held on to everything but that which was beautiful. There, I realized that my broken self was in need of a healer—one who would free me from the captivity of myself.

At every juncture of grief where my spirit was cracked to the point of no return came an experience that mended it back together, reminding me that these survivors were the leaders I've been waiting for. It became very clear to me that those who have experienced oppression could be the ones to lead us all into liberation. Through their stories, their wisdom, their experiences of pain and their models of love, survivors have the potential to become the most powerful liberators in our midst.

"My scars are evidence that wounds do heal," Mubanga frequently tells me as she shows me the scars on her wrists. When my anxiety is high, when the pain of this world is too heavy to hold, when my desire to control outcomes toward justice are met with failure, I am reminded that she is evidence of healing. If our bodies can heal physically, perhaps our invisible wounds will one day be healed as well.

Redemption is hidden in the most unexpected places—in brokenness, in pain, in despair, in suffering, because those are the places where love's presence is necessary. Just as light coexists with darkness to make a photograph visible, the juxtaposition of seemingly opposing attributes can expand the capacity of our heart.

Pain expands our capacity for joy by deepening our heart's ability to experience a broader spectrum of emotion, both pain and joy together. Without pain, we wouldn't know what joy could be.

While I was working hard to heal their broken hearts, I found that their courageous lives were actually healing mine.

For where there is pain,
there is an abundance of joy.

Where there is brokenness,
there is mysterious beauty.

Where there is despair,
there is always hope.

Where there is suffering,
there is love.

nineteen

HERE AM I

MARA-ANNE AND I EVEN-TUALLY took our message internationally, with our first stop in Spain. We were invited to Barcelona to train artists on using art to bring healing to survivors of sexual violence. This trip would be Mara-Anne's very first plane ride.

At Jomo Kenyatta International Airport, there were no seats in the waiting area, so we sat on the floor as we waited for our gate to open. "I can't believe this," she exclaimed while staring at her ticket. "When I was young, I wanted to be a pilot so that I could fly away from the mess that I knew in Kibera. But then I ended up on the streets." She shook her head in disbelief. "Imagine! I could have been on this same airplane in the cargo, flying to God knows where because I had no choice. But now I'm flying by choice, because I want to. I'm doing work that I absolutely love. My ticket even has a seat number on it!" She looked at her ticket as if it had turned to gold. "If I could be grateful for anything during my time in that brothel, was that the pimp got me this passport. She would never believe that I am using this same passport to share my story of hope in Barcelona instead of pros-tituting in brothels in America."

When we boarded, I made sure she had a window seat. She sat down and exclaimed, "Look! I'm sitting in my seat!" When we took off, she clutched my hand and covered her eyes. "You have to look down at Nairobi as we leave!" I told her. She slid her hand from her eyes to her mouth, muffling squeals of excitement. When we travel together, we often get ourselves into trouble for being too loud, laughing from the gut. The people sitting in front of us turned around to glare at us. We shushed each other, which only made us laugh harder. They could never understand the reason for our uncontainable happiness.

As we leveled out, she turned to me and in all seriousness asked, "When you go to the bathroom on the plane, does your poop fall on people's heads? I always cover my head when I see an airplane flying over."

"Go find out yourself," I smirked while pointing to the back.

"Oh my goodness, the bathroom is so far. This plane is too big. I have to walk to the other side of town to get there."

When she came back, her eyes were big with her newfound discovery.

"I feel like Obama—I am the only black person on the plane!"

The day after we arrived in Barcelona, she wanted to watch the planes take off. We found a front-row seat along the sea point and watched the planes come in to land in staggered pairs of two. Each landing was met with oohs and aahs from Mara-Anne's childlike wonderment. Not only was she living her dream of being in a country outside of Africa, I was living my dream of cofacilitating programs with a survivor in international spaces. She sparked this dream while in Kisumu just a few years before, and today, it was landing in reality.

As she looked into the sky, she thought of her nieces and how she wanted them to have even better opportunities than she. She wanted them to live in a world where they would finally be free.

"Just before I came, something happened at home. My niece— you know, she's almost eleven now? Ghai! I can't believe how much she has grown, my first baby. Anyway, I told her to take out the trash. It was at night. The trash is burned just outside the gate, so you don't have to go far. The watchman grabbed her and dragged her into his guard post. She screamed and screamed. I've trained my nieces for this, telling them if anyone touches them they must fight for their lives. The neighbors came, and they beat up the watchman until he was almost dead. Heh! I almost died. Good thing the neighbors beat him up, otherwise I would have definitely killed him myself. I felt so bad for making her take the trash out at night. I will never do that again."

I exhaled, wondering when all of our girls in the world will finally be free. Mara-Anne wanted to count the number of planes landing in honor of the travels she would have on this round trip—four plane rides. As the planes came in by pairs, she counted each one, cheering for the grit and grace that brought her this far.

As we watched the last two planes come in to land, the plane trailing behind the other one caught up and surpassed the plane in front. Mara-Anne jumped up and down. "Look at this last plane overtaking the one in front! It is true that the least shall be greatest!" She hugged me while jumping up and down. We keeled over because our bellies hurt from laughter.

◆ ❈ ◆

In Barcelona, the mom of a friend invited us to go with her to bring coffee and cookies to the women working on the streets Las Ramblas.

Mara-Anne had been excited about this all week. She took a nap after teaching that day to emotionally prepare for what was to come. When I came to wake her up, she rolled over and refused to get up. The thought of intentionally going into the hell she'd lived in before was far too much to bear. "You've been looking forward to this all week. Remember why you're here," I firmly reminded her. In coming to Barcelona, Mara-Anne was adamant about meeting women who had been trafficked through prostitution. Because she was spared from being trafficked, she knew her purpose was to bring hope to women who hadn't been as lucky as she. We left to take the train to Las Ramblas.

We met with our friend's mom, who didn't speak a word of English. I communicated with her in my terribly broken Spanish. She told us that women on the streets are predominantly African and Chinese; the trafficked women of Las Ramblas look exactly like Mara-Anne and me.

She told us that many of these girls on the streets come here through traffickers masquerading as boyfriends. It broke her heart, seeing how much these girls longed for love yet found themselves trapped in exploitation. She told us that their situations are complex and it was unsafe for her to get too close to them. She wished with all her heart that she could pull them all out and bring them home with her, but she couldn't. The only thing she could do was to chat with them over coffee and cookies. She was grateful that we came with her to communicate with the girls in English, since their Spanish was limited. I could only nod and respond, "Vale," to convey that I understood. I wanted to tell her how much I often felt that way too—that even as much as I try to bring our girls into safe places, I cannot save them from the violence of this world. It took a while to construct all that I wanted to say in my limited Spanish. All I could think of was, "Tu amor y presencia es muy importante." As I told her this, it was also a reminder to myself that our loving presence is most important. We can only pray that one day our intent will lead to their freedom. She sighed with relief and responded, "Si, espero que si."

As Mara-Anne and I walked along Las Ramblas, Barcelona's famous shopping street, I looked at the faces in the crowd. European shoppers passed by glowing window displays full of shiny objects, while others lurked in the darkness of back alleys. These back alleys were full—not of fancy window displays—but of the stench of piss in the streets, of little girls with Nokia cellphones and men holding cash with dirty hands. Their hollow eyes stared at us as if we were corpses, slowly brushing past our bodies, whispering profanities in our ears. A man approached Mara-Anne and asked, "Hey sweetie, are you working?"

She firmly yelled back at him, "No!" I pulled her close. I could feel her anger rising. Flashbacks of almost losing her once before came over me—for there were too many times that she didn't know that she had the option to say "no." I held her even tighter to keep our arms from throwing punches.

Even in my rage, I thought, *how beautiful that she can now say "no," that she is stronger than he is, that she can save herself, that she is ready to fight back, that she is intentionally going back into the darkness to reclaim her redemption.*

A moment later, a little Nigerian girl walked up to us. She was barely five feet tall. I poured her coffee and Mara-Anne talked to her. I watched their interaction in awe. How beautiful it is that the one who could not recognize the power of her voice is now reminding the other to listen to the inner voice within, that the one who didn't know she was a warrior is now fighting for the other's safety, that the one who is now liberated is tirelessly liberating others around her.

As I witnessed the beauty of this interaction, the little girl's Nokia cellphone rang. She thanked us for the coffee. With a look of empathy, Mara-Anne gave her a warm hug and didn't want to let her go. The little girl walked down the street, met a man much older and taller than she, and entered into the brothel. The doors closed behind her.

There was agony in Mara-Anne's eyes as she followed the steps of that little Nigerian girl who was now imprisoned in a place that Mara-Anne knew far too well. And I knew what she was thinking—that the little Nigerian girl could have been her. In that warm embrace were all the prayers of hope, dreams held in secret, and words of strength that she needed for herself when she was that age.

Mara-Anne had given a hug to another version of herself. Her name was Faith.

We met two more Nigerian women. Their laughter echoed throughout the streets. One woman was named Blessing and the other Loveth. Their laughter was contagious and confusing; perhaps laughter was the only way to cope with despair. Laughter became our common language that spoke life beyond any words we could ever offer. After exchanging what semblance of happiness we could, Mara-Anne offered to pray for them—for their peace of mind, their safety on these streets, and for their children back in Nigeria.

Before Mara-Anne could say "amen," a man came from behind and forcefully grabbed her arm. Blessing yelled at him, "Don't bother her! Can't you see that we are praying! God is not pleased with you! The fire of God is coming down to smite you! Fire! Fire!"

Mara-Anne was saved, this time by one who was not yet freed. Again I thought how beautiful that the one still in bondage is able to defend her, that the one without an advocate is advocating for her, that the one who has not yet been liberated knows what liberation could look like for herself.

That night, I listened to Mara-Anne breathing heavily as she slept on the bunk bed below me. I reeled through memories of all our adventures together and the unexpected gifts found along the way. I couldn't help but smile into the darkness staring back at me. Through this work, I found liberation from bondage I didn't realize I was in. My desire to control the outcomes of my work limited me from experiencing something more, beyond that which I could control. As I limited my ability to feel, I also limited my heart's capacity to hold the world's suffering.

But liberation comes as the heart expands, allowing pain and joy, grief and hope, brokenness and beauty to coexist. Liberation comes as we recognize our shared humanity, and how dignity cannot be taken away by poverty, violence, or oppression, but it is an inherent gift from God. Liberation comes in the collective pursuit of justice, moving the power of my leadership into the hands of those who have been liberated.

I found it in Nekesa, whose story compelled me to identify with an experience of trauma not my own. In it, I found liberation from ignorance that there was something greater than I've experienced before.

I found it in Mara-Anne, who taught me to be unafraid of my voice, for sharing our story allows us to shed light into the darkness. I found liberation by intentionally going back into the darkness to reclaim my redemption.

I found it in Mubanga, who taught me to practice gentleness in a violent world so that I do not inflict the violence in myself on others. I found liberation from my impulse to fight, allowing the process of healing to take place.

I found it in Amani, who boldly seeks after justice, not only for herself but also for the many girls she represents. I found liberation by clinging to hope—believing that justice comes in many forms.

I found it in Ruby, whose spirit-filled voice, despite the labels placed on her, challenges me to live a life of courage. I found liberation from the ways in which I place oppressive labels on myself.

I found it in Akinyi, who boldly seeks after justice, not only for herself but also for the many girls she represents. I found liberation by clinging to hope—believing that justice comes in many forms.

I found it in Faith, Loveth, Blessing, and the multitudes of women still under the weight of oppression. I found liberation in releasing the many things that I cannot control.

That night, I rested, knowing that we were saved not by ourselves but by the voice of a woman in prostitution.

"Here am I," she seemed to say, "for our liberation is bound to each other."

*May our liberation come as we seek
to bring liberation to others, realizing
that our freedoms are bound together
in our common humanity.*

*May our pain expand our capacity
for joy, our brokenness lead to
realizations of beauty within, our
despair challenge us to cling to hope,
and our suffering invite us to love.*

*May we realize that God's presence
is found in the voices of the
oppressed among us.*

*May we learn to love ourselves as
we love the oppressed in our world,
inviting us into an experience of
liberation that is nearer to us
than ever before.*

ACKNOWLEDGMENTS

I OWE MY DEEPEST GRATITUDE to survivors of sexual violence who exhibit great courage, power, and strength. You are the embodiment of hope. Your voices matter, and I believe you.

Thank you to InterVarsity Press and Angela Scheff for taking the leap into this creative project.

Mahtem Shiferraw, Rebecca Crook, and Lovelyn Nwadeyi, thank you for your meaningful edits, for inspiring me with your vocations, and for challenging me to be better in mine.

Auntie Lisa and Uncle David, you have provided healing space, honest conversation, life-giving laughter, and renewing time to move toward all that I aspire to create. Every moment you've invested in me has formed my leadership trajectory. Thank you for reminding me to trust this difficult process, for enduring my outrageous outbursts, and for guiding me closer to who I desire to become. Thank you for not allowing me to give up on this work that I love so much.

To my mentors Chiraphone Khampouvong, Rudy Rasmus, and Romal Tune, you have inspired me to write, utilize my voice, and find rest when my body needed it most. I am deeply grateful for your mentorship in this writing process and for advocating for me in countless ways. Your examples have saved my faith.

To my friends who have encouraged me to put these transformative experiences into words, you believed in me before I believed in myself: Sha' Givens, Koko Yee, Jen Arens, Janai Marshall, Jenny Phrasavath, Rachel Goble, Ying Guo, and Anahi Salazar. To Dwayne and Janet Betsill, Bud and Elaine Smith, and Candice Bond, thank you for providing the space for me to heal through writing.

My work is made possible through my incredible staff across Kenya and Zambia, who fearlessly fight for this audacious mission of ending sexual violence. To my board, who allowed me the time and creative space to write. To our fellows, scholars, and survivor-leaders, who have formed this organization through your prophetic vision and awe-inspiring determination to form a more beautiful and just world.

To Gung Gung, my parents, and my sister, who have supported this dream without fully knowing the effect that it would have on our relationships, finances, distance, and communion. To my grandparents and ancestors who have persisted through racism, poverty, and political oppression to create liberating opportunities for me and my generation. Thank you for giving me the blessing to pursue a dream that has become much bigger than my own.

To my Powerhouse, I am forever grateful for your generous, honest, and understanding spirit that has taught me to be a better ally. Thank you for correcting and challenging me—helping me become the woman I aspire to be. This, my heart's work, is for you and for the many others that your story represents. I love you most, moster, mostest.

To Freely in Hope's global community of survivors of sexual violence, who have invited me into your stories. Thank you for allowing me into your innermost thoughts, your darkest pains, and your audacious dreams. This book was made possible through your friendship and patient love. Everything I know about healing, redemption, and hope is through you.

GLOSSARY

asante (Swahili): Thank you.

avafumu (Swahili): Medicine men or witch doctors who practice indigenous medicine in Kenya.

boda boda (Luhya): A taxi motorbike.

bwino (Nyanja): Fine.

chai (Swahili): Black tea mixed with milk and sugar. Tea is a large export product of Kenya.

chang'aa (Swahili) or **busaa** (Luhya): Meaning "kill me quickly," chang'aa is a home-brewed spirit made from fermented grains, often laced with petrol oil or embalming fluid.

cheka (Swahili): Smile or laugh.

eshitwatsi (Luhya): A derogatory term meaning "prostitute."

eywe (Luhya): A term often used at the beginning of the sentence to call attention to or to address someone. It literally means "you."

ghai! (Swahili): An expression of shock or surprise commonly heard in Nairobi.

githeri (Swahili): A dish made of beans and maize common in the Kikuyu and Kamba tribes.

ifisashi (Bemba): A dish consisting of vegetable leaves boiled down and boiled with freshly roasted groundnuts pounded into a powder.

jiko (Swahili): A small stove about one foot tall, made of metal. The jiko has two compartments: the bottom tray holds the fire, and the top tray holds the charcoal on which the sufuria is placed.

jook (Cantonese): Rice porridge or conjee made by boiling rice and water.

kalindula: A traditional bass guitar, which gives its name to a style of popular music in southern-central Africa. It originated in the late twentieth century and is popular in Zambia.

kapenta (Nyanja) or **omena** (Swahili): Sun-dried sardines. They are cooked dry in oil or with a sauce made of tomatoes and onions.

karibu (Swahili): Welcome.

kitenge (Swahili) or **chitenge** (Nyanja): African fabric with designs full of bright colors printed using a traditional batik technique. It is used by women to carry babies on their backs, to tie around their waists, or as celebratory banners. The fabric is also used for tailor-made clothes.

kwacha (Tonga): Zambian currency. The exchange rate is about 12 kwacha to $1 US dollar.

Lei sik jor faan mei ah? (Cantonese): Have you eaten yet?

mandazi (Swahili): Also known as beignets or fritters, mandazi is a common breakfast food made with self-rising flour, hand-molded into small pillows, and deep fried.

matatu (Swahili): The local fourteen-passenger van that provides public transportation. Matatu drivers are known to be hostile on the road.

mbaula (Nyanja): An mbaula is a small stove, about one foot high, that is made of clay or aluminum. Charcoal is lit at the base as heat for cooking.

mopane worms: Mopane worms, known as ifishimu in Bemba, are dried and eaten as a snack or rehydrated in water and fried with tomatoes and onions.

mrenda (Luhya): Also known as jute mallow or molokhia, mrenda is a traditional vegetable grown mostly in the western part of Kenya.

mshino (Swahili): Kenyan slang for tinsel, often draped over the necks of graduates.

Muli bwanji? (Nyanja): How are you?

mzungu (Swahili): Foreigner.

Ndiri bwino. Kaya inu? (Nyanja): I'm fine. And you?

nshima or **ugali**: A staple food in Zambia and Kenya, nshima is made from processed corn meal, boiled with water, and stirred into a thick substance. It is eaten with your hands and scooped together with the dish accompanying it.

nsolo (Nyanja): Also known as mancala, nsolo is a game played by scooping rows of holes in the ground and using stones for playing pieces.

pamoja (Swahili): Together.

pídàn (Cantonese): Also known as a thousand-year-old egg, pídàn is a fermented egg.

Qi Gong (Chinese): A Chinese practice involving movement, breathing, and meditation that seeks to bring the body to holistic health.

shillings (Swahili): Kenyan currency. The exchange rate is about 100 shillings to $1 USD.

Si, espero que si (Spanish): Yes, I hope so.

sufuria (Swahili): An aluminum pot.

sukuma wiki (Swahili): Also known as collard greens. In Swahili the name literally means "stretch the week," because it is an affordable vegetable that is available year-round.

Tu amor y presencia es muy importante (Spanish): Your love and presence is more important.

Tuko pamoja? (Swahili): Are we together?

vale (Spanish): Okay.

About
FREELY IN HOPE

FREELY IN HOPE IS A 501(c)(3) nonprofit organization dedicated to equipping survivors and advocates to lead in ending the cycle of sexual violence. Our programs provide holistic education, leadership development, and storytelling platforms allowing survivors of sexual violence to lead through their rewritten stories. Working across Kenya and Zambia, we fund high school and university scholarships, safe housing, health care, and mental health support. We train on transformative leadership development models and have survivor-led and -designed outreach programs that aim to prevent sexual violence. We believe that survivors of sexual violence have the potential to become the most powerful leaders in our community.

Learn more at freelyinhope.org.